THE QUAKER COLONIES

TEXTBOOK EDITION

∴

THE CHRONICLES OF AMERICA SERIES
ALLEN JOHNSON
EDITOR

GERHARD R. LOMER
CHARLES W. JEFFERYS
ASSISTANT EDITORS

THE QUAKER COLONIES

A CHRONICLE OF THE
PROPRIETORS OF THE DELAWARE
BY SYDNEY G. FISHER

NEW HAVEN: YALE UNIVERSITY PRESS
TORONTO: GLASGOW, BROOK & CO.
LONDON: HUMPHREY MILFORD
OXFORD UNIVERSITY PRESS

CONTENTS

CONTENTS

THE QUAKER COLONIES

∴

CHAPTER I

In 1661, the year after Charles II was restored to the throne of England, William Penn was a seventeen-year-old student at Christ Church, Oxford. His father, a distinguished admiral in high favor at Court, had abandoned his erstwhile friends and had aided in restoring King Charlie to his own again. Young William was associating with the sons of the aristocracy and was receiving an education which would fit him to obtain preferment at Court. But there was a serious vein in him, and while at a high church Oxford College he was surreptitiously attending the meetings and listening to the preaching of the despised and outlawed Quakers. There he first began to hear of the plans of a group of Quakers to found colonies on the

1

Delaware in America. Forty years afterwards he wrote, "I had an opening of joy as to these parts in the year 1661 at Oxford." And with America and the Quakers, in spite of a brief youthful experience as a soldier and a courtier, William Penn's life, as well as his fame, is indissolubly linked.

Quakerism was one of the many religious sects born in the seventeenth century under the influence of Puritan thought. The foundation principle of the Reformation, the right of private judgment, the Quakers carried out to its logical conclusion; but they were people whose minds had so long been suppressed and terrorized that, once free, they rushed to extremes. They shocked and horrified even the most advanced Reformation sects by rejecting Baptism, the doctrine of the Trinity, and all sacraments, forms, and ceremonies. They represented, on their best side, the most vigorous effort of the Reformation to return to the spirituality and the simplicity of the early Christians. But their intense spirituality, pathetic often in its extreme manifestations, was not wholly concerned with another world. Their humane ideas and philanthropic methods, such as the abolition of slavery, and the reform of prisons and of charitable institutions, came in time to be accepted as fundamental practical social principles.

The tendencies of which Quakerism formed only one manifestation appeared outside of England, in Italy, in France, and especially in Germany. The fundamental Quaker idea of "quietism," as it was called, or peaceful, silent contemplation as a spiritual form of worship and as a development of moral consciousness, was very widespread at the close of the Reformation and even began to be practiced in the Roman Catholic Church until it was stopped by the Jesuits. The most extreme of the English Quakers, however, gave way to such extravagances of conduct as trembling when they preached (whence their name), preaching openly in the streets and fields — a horrible thing at that time — interrupting other congregations, and appearing naked as a sign and warning. They gave offense by refusing to remove their hats in public and by applying to all alike the words "thee" and "thou," a form of address hitherto used only to servants and inferiors. Worst of all, the Quakers refused to pay tithes or taxes to support the Church of England. As a result, the loathsome jails of the day were soon filled with these objectors, and their property melted away

in fines. This contumacy and their street meetings, regarded at that time as riotous breaches of
the peace, gave the Government at first a legal
excuse to hunt them down; but as they grew in
numbers and influence, laws were enacted to suppress them. Some of them, though not the wild-
est extremists, escaped to the colonies in America. There, however, they were made welcome to
conditions no less severe.

The first law against the Quakers in Massachusetts was passed in 1656, and between that date
and 1660 four of the sect were hanged, one of them
a woman, Mary Dyer. Though there were no
other hangings, many Quakers were punished
by whipping and banishment. In other colonies,
notably New York, fines and banishment were not
uncommon. Such treatment forced the Quakers,
against the will of many of them, to seek a tract
of land and found a colony of their own. To such
a course there appeared no alternative, unless they
were determined to establish their religion solely
by martyrdom.

About the time when the Massachusetts laws
were enforced, the principal Quaker leader and
organizer, George Fox (1624–1691), began to
consider the possibility of making a settlement

among the great forests and mountains said to lie north of Maryland in the region drained by the Delaware and Susquehanna rivers. In this region lay practically the only good land on the Atlantic seaboard not already occupied. The Puritans and Dutch were on the north, and there were Catholic and Church of England colonies on the south in Maryland and Virginia. The middle ground was unoccupied because heretofore a difficult coast had prevented easy access by sea. Fox consulted Josiah Coale, a Quaker who had traveled in America and had seen a good deal of the Indian tribes, with the result that on his second visit to America Coale was commissioned to treat with the Susquehanna Indians, who were supposed to have rights in the desired land. In November, 1660, Coale reported to Fox the result of his inquiries: "As concerning Friends buying a piece of land of the Susquehanna Indians I have spoken of it to them and told them what thou said concerning it; but their answer was, that there is no land that is habitable or fit for situation beyond Baltimore's liberty till they come to or near the Susquehanna's Fort."[1] Nothing could be done

[1] James Bowden's *History of the Friends in America*, vol. I, p. 389.

immediately, the letter went on to say, because
the Indians were at war with one another, and William Fuller, a Maryland Quaker, whose coöperation
was deemed essential, was absent.

This seems to have been the first definite movement towards a Quaker colony. Reports of it
reached the ears of young Penn at Oxford and set
his imagination aflame. He never forgot the project, for seventeen is an age when grand thoughts
strike home. The adventurousness of the plan
was irresistible — a home for the new faith in
the primeval forest, far from imprisonment, tithes,
and persecution, and to be won by effort worthy of
a man. It was, however, a dream destined not
to be realized for many a long year. More was
needed than the mere consent of the Indians. In
the meantime, however, a temporary refuge for
the sect was found in the province of West Jersey
on the Delaware, which two Quakers had bought
from Lord Berkeley for the comparatively small
sum of £1000. Of this grant William Penn became one of the trustees and thus gained his first
experience in the business of colonizing the region
of his youthful dreams. But there was never a
sufficient governmental control of West Jersey to
make it an ideal Quaker colony. What little

control the Quakers exercised disappeared after 1702; and the land and situation were not all that could be desired. Penn, though also one of the owners of East Jersey, made no attempt to turn that region into a Quaker colony.

Besides West Jersey the Quakers found a temporary asylum in Aquidneck, now Rhode Island.[1] For many years the governors and magistrates were Quakers, and the affairs of this island colony were largely in their hands. Quakers were also prominent in the politics of North Carolina, and John Archdale, a Quaker, was Governor for several years. They formed a considerable element of the population in the towns of Long Island and Westchester County but they could not hope to convert these communities into real Quaker commonwealths.

The experience in the Jerseys and elsewhere very soon proved that if there was to be a real Quaker colony, the British Crown must give not only a title to the land but a strong charter guaranteeing self-government and protection of the Quaker faith from outside interference. But that

[1] This Rhode Island colony should be distinguished from the settlement at Providence founded by Roger Williams with which it was later united. See Jones, *The Quakers in the American Colonies*, p. 21, note.

the British Government would grant such valued privileges to a sect of schismatics which it was hunting down in England seemed a most unlikely event. Nothing but unusual influence at Court could bring it about, and in that quarter the Quakers had no influence.

Penn never forgot the boyhood ideal which he had developed at college. For twenty years he led a varied life — driven from home and whipped by his father for consorting with the schismatics; sometimes in deference to his father's wishes taking his place in the gay world at Court; even, for a time, becoming a soldier, and again traveling in France with some of the people of the Court. In the end, as he grew older, religious feeling completely absorbed him. He became one of the leading Quaker theologians, and his very earnest religious writings fill several volumes. He became a preacher at the meetings and went to prison for his heretical doctrines and pamphlets. At last he found himself at the age of thirty-six with his father dead, and a debt due from the Crown of £16,000 for services which his distinguished father, the admiral, had rendered the Government.

Here was the accident that brought into being the great Quaker colony, by a combination of circumstances which could hardly have happened twice. Young Penn was popular at Court. He had inherited a valuable friendship with Charles II and his heir, the Duke of York. This friendship rested on the solid fact that Penn's father, the admiral, had rendered such signal assistance in restoring Charles and the whole Stuart line to the throne. But still £16,000 or $80,000, the accumulation of many deferred payments, was a goodly sum in those days, and that the Crown would pay it in money, of which it had none too much, was unlikely. Why not therefore suggest paying it instead in wild land in America, of which the Crown had abundance? That was the fruitful thought which visited Penn. Lord Berkeley and Lord Carteret had been given New Jersey because they had signally helped to restore the Stuart family to the throne. All the more therefore should the Stuart family give a tract of land, and even a larger tract, to Penn, whose father had not only assisted the family to the throne but had refrained so long from pressing his just claim for money due.

So the Crown, knowing little of the value of it, granted him the most magnificent domain of mountains, lakes, rivers, and forests, fertile soil,

coal, petroleum, and iron that ever was given to
a single proprietor. In addition to giving Penn
the control of Delaware and, with certain other
Quakers, that of New Jersey as well, the Crown
placed at the disposal of the Quakers 55,000 square
miles of most valuable, fertile territory, lacking
only about three thousand square miles of being
as large as England and Wales. Even when cut
down to 45,000 square miles by a boundary dispute with Maryland, it was larger than Ireland.
Kings themselves have possessed such dominions,
but never before a private citizen who scorned all
titles and belonged to a hunted sect that exalted
peace and spiritual contemplation above all the
wealth and power of the world. Whether the obtaining of this enormous tract of the best land in
America was due to what may be called the eternal
thriftiness of the Quaker mind or to the intense desire of the British Government to get rid of these
people at any cost might be hard to determine.

Penn received his charter in 1681, and in it he
was very careful to avoid all the mistakes of the
Jersey proprietary grants. Instead of numerous
proprietors, Penn was to be the sole proprietor.
Instead of giving title to the land and remaining silent about the political government, Penn's

charter not only gave him title to the land but a clearly defined position as its political head, and described the principles of the government so clearly that there was little room for doubt or dispute.

It was a decidedly feudal charter, very much like the one granted to Lord Baltimore fifty years before, and yet at the same time it secured civil liberty and representative government to the people. Penn owned all the land and the colonists were to be his tenants. He was compelled, however, to give his people free government. The laws were to be made by him with the assent of the people or their delegates. In practice this of course meant that the people were to elect a legislature and Penn would have a veto, as we now call it, on such acts as the legislature should pass. He had power to appoint magistrates, judges, and some other officers, and to grant pardons. Though by the charter proprietor of the province, he usually remained in England and appointed a deputy governor to exercise authority in the colony. In modern phrase, he controlled the executive part of the government and his people controlled the legislative part.

Pennsylvania, besides being the largest in area of the proprietary colonies, was also the most successful, not only from the proprietor's point of view but also from the point of view of the inhabitants. The proprietorships in Maine, New Hampshire, New Jersey, and the Carolinas were largely failures. Maryland was only partially successful; it was not particularly remunerative to its owner, and the Crown deprived him of his control of it for twenty years. Penn, too, was deprived of the control of Pennsylvania by William III but for only about two years. Except for this brief interval (1692–1694), Penn and his sons after him held their province down to the time of the American Revolution in 1776, a period of ninety-four years.

A feudal proprietorship, collecting rents from all the people, seems to modern minds grievously wrong in theory, and yet it would be very difficult to show that it proved onerous in practice. Under it the people of Pennsylvania flourished in wealth, peace, and happiness. Penn won undying fame for the liberal principles of his feudal enterprise. His expenses in England were so great and his quitrents always so much in arrears that he was seldom out of debt. But his children grew rich from the province. As in other provinces that were not feudal there were disputes between the people and the proprietors; but there was not so much general dissatisfaction as might have been expected. The proprietors were on the whole not altogether disliked. In the American Revolution, when the people could have confiscated everything in Pennsylvania belonging to the proprietary family, they not only left them in possession of a large part of their land, but paid them handsomely for the part that was taken.

After Penn had secured his charter in 1681, he obtained from the Duke of York the land now included in the State of Delaware. He advertised for colonists, and began selling land at £100 for five thousand acres and annually thereafter a shilling quitrent for every hundred acres. He drew up a constitution or frame of government, as he called it, after wide and earnest consultation with many, including the famous Algernon Sydney. Among the Penn papers in the Historical Society of Pennsylvania is a collection of about twenty preliminary drafts. Beginning with one which created a government by a landed aristocracy, they became more and more liberal, until in the end his frame was very much like the most liberal government of the other English colonies in America. He had a council and an assembly, both

elected by the people. The council, however, was
very large, had seventy-two members, and was
more like an upper house of the Legislature than
the usual colonial governor's council. The council also had the sole right of proposing legislation, and the assembly could merely accept or
reject its proposals. This was a new idea, and
it worked so badly in practice that in the end
the province went to the opposite extreme and
had no council or upper house of the Legislature
at all.

Penn's frame of government contained, however,
a provision for its own amendment. This was a
new idea and proved to be so happy that it is now
found in all American constitutions. His method
of impeachment by which the lower house was to
bring in the charge and the upper house was to
try it has also been universally adopted. His view
that an unconstitutional law is void was a step
towards our modern system. The next step, giving the courts power to declare a law unconstitutional, was not taken until one hundred years
after his time. With the advice and assistance
of some of those who were going out to his colony
he prepared a code of laws which contained many
of the advanced ideas of the Quakers. Capital

punishment was to be confined to murder and treason, instead of being applied as in England to a host of minor offenses. The property of murderers, instead of being forfeited to the State, was to be divided among the next of kin of the victim and of the criminal. Religious liberty was established as it had been in Rhode Island and the Jerseys. All children were to be taught a useful trade. Oaths in judicial proceedings were not required. All prisons were to be workhouses and places of reformation instead of dungeons of dirt, idleness, and disease. This attempt to improve the prisons inaugurated a movement of great importance in the modern world in which the part played by the Quakers is too often forgotten.

Penn had now started his "Holy Experiment," as he called his enterprise in Pennsylvania, by which he intended to prove that religious liberty was not only right, but that agriculture, commerce, and all arts and refinements of life would flourish under it. He would break the delusion that prosperity and morals were possible only under some one particular faith established by law. He would prove that government could be carried on without war and without oaths, and that primitive Christianity could be maintained without a hireling ministry, without persecution, without ridiculous dogmas or ritual, sustained only by its own innate power and the inward light.

CHAPTER II

THE framing of the constitution and other preparations consumed the year following Penn's receipt of his charter in 1681. But at last, on August 30, 1682, he set sail in the ship *Welcome*, with about a hundred colonists. After a voyage of about six weeks, and the loss of thirty of their number by smallpox, they arrived in the Delaware. June would have been a somewhat better month in which to see the rich luxuriance of the green meadows and forests of this beautiful river. But the autumn foliage and bracing air of October must have been inspiring enough. The ship slowly beat her way for three days up the bay and river in the silence and romantic loneliness of its shores. Everything indicated richness and fertility. At some points the lofty trees of the primeval forest grew down to the water's edge. The river at every high tide overflowed great meadows grown

2   17

up in reeds and grasses and red and yellow flowers, stretching back to the borders of the forest and full of water birds and wild fowl of every variety. Penn, now in the prime of life, must surely have been aroused by this scene and by the reflection that the noble river was his and the vast stretches of forests and mountains for three hundred miles to the westward.

He was soon ashore, exploring the edge of his mighty domain, settling his government, and passing his laws. He was much pleased with the Swedes whom he found on his land. He changed the name of the little Swedish village of Upland, fifteen miles below Philadelphia, to Chester. He superintended laying out the streets of Philadelphia and they remain to this day substantially as he planned them, though unfortunately too narrow and monotonously regular. He met the Indians at Philadelphia, sat with them at their fires, ate their roasted corn, and when to amuse him they showed him some of their sports and games he renewed his college days by joining them in a jumping match.

Then he started on journeys. He traveled through the woods to New York, which then belonged to the Duke of York, who had given him

Delaware; he visited the Long Island Quakers; and on his return he went to Maryland to meet with much pomp and ceremony Lord Baltimore and there discuss with him the disputed boundary. He even crossed to the eastern shore of the Chesapeake to visit a Quaker meeting on the Choptank before winter set in, and he describes the immense migration of wild pigeons at that season, and the flocks which flew so low and were so tame that the colonists knocked them down with sticks.

Most of the winter he spent at Chester and wrote to England in high spirits of his journeys, the wonders of the country, the abundance of game and provisions, and the twenty-three ships which had arrived so swiftly that few had taken longer than six weeks, and only three had been infected with the smallpox. "Oh how sweet," he says, "is the quiet of these parts, freed from the anxious and troublesome solicitations, hurries and perplexities of woful Europe."

As the weeks and months passed, ships kept arriving with more Quakers, far exceeding the migration to the Jerseys. By summer, Penn reported that 50 sail had arrived within the past year, 80 houses had been built in Philadelphia, and about 300 farms had been laid out round the

town.   It is supposed that about 3000 immigrants
had arrived.   This was a more rapid development
than was usual in the colonies of America.   Massachusetts and Virginia had been established slowly
and with much privation and suffering. But the
settlement of Philadelphia was like a summer out-
ing. There were no dangers, the hardships were tri-
fling, and there was no sickness or famine.   There
was such an abundance of game close at hand that
hunger and famine were in nowise to be feared.
The climate was good and the Indians, kindly
treated, remained friendly for seventy years.

It is interesting to note that in that same year,
1682, in which Penn and his friends with such ease
and comfort founded their great colony on the
Delaware, the French explorers and *voyageurs* from
Canada, after years of incredible hardships, had
traversed the northern region of the Great Lakes
with their canoes and had passed down the Mississippi to its mouth, giving to the whole of the
Great West the name of Louisiana, and claiming
it for France.   Already La Salle had taken his
fleet of canoes down the Mississippi River and
had placed the arms of France on a post at its
mouth in April, 1682, only a few months before
Penn reached his newly acquired colony.   Thus

in the same year in which the Quakers established in Pennsylvania their reign of liberty and of peace with the red men, La Salle was laying the foundation of the western empire of despotic France, which seventy years afterwards was to hurl the savages upon the English colonies, to wreck the Quaker policy of peace, but to fail in the end to maintain itself against the free colonies of England.

While they were building houses in Philadelphia, the settlers lived in bark huts or in caves dug in the river bank, as the early settlers in New Jersey across the river had lived. Pastorius, a learned German Quaker, who had come out with the English, placed over the door of his cave the motto, "*Parva domus, sed amica bonis, procul este profani,*" which much amused Penn when he saw it. A certain Mrs. Morris was much exercised one day as to how she could provide supper in the cave for her husband who was working on the construction of their house. But on returning to her cave she found that her cat had just brought in a fine rabbit. In their later prosperous years they had a picture of the cat and the rabbit made on a box which has descended as a family heirloom. Doubtless there were preserved many other interesting reminiscences of the brief camp life.

These Quakers were all of the thrifty, industrious type which had gone to West Jersey a few years before. Men of means, indeed, among the Quakers were the first to seek refuge from the fines and confiscations imposed upon them in England. They brought with them excellent supplies of everything. Many of the ships carried the frames of houses ready to put together. But substantial people of this sort demanded for the most part houses of brick, with stone cellars. Fortunately both brick clay and stone were readily obtainable in the neighborhood, and whatever may have been the case in other colonies, ships loaded with brick from England would have found it little to their profit to touch at Philadelphia. An early description says that the brick houses in Philadelphia were modeled on those of London, and this type prevailed for nearly two hundred years.

It was probably in June, 1683, that Penn made his famous treaty with the Indians. No documentary proof of the existence of such a treaty has reached us. He made, indeed, a number of so-called treaties, which were really only purchases of land involving oral promises between the principals to treat each other fairly. Hundreds of such treaties have been made. The remarkable

part about Penn's dealings with the Indians was
that such promises as he made he kept.   The
other Quakers, too, were as careful as Penn in
their honorable treatment of the red men.   Quaker families of farmers and settlers lived unarmed
among them for generations and, when absent
from home, left children in their care.   The Indians, on their part, were known to have helped
white families with food in winter time.   Penn,
on his first visit to the colony, made a long journey
unarmed among the Indians as far as the Susquehanna, saw the great herds of elk on that river,
lived in Indian wigwams, and learned much of
the language and customs of the natives.   There
need never be any trouble with them, he said.
They were the easiest people in the world to get
on with if the white men would simply be just.
Penn's fair treatment of the Indians kept Pennsylvania at peace with them for about seventy
years — in fact, from 1682 until the outbreak
of the French and Indian Wars, in 1755.   In its
critical period of growth, Pennsylvania was therefore not at all harassed or checked by those Indian
hostilities which were such a serious impediment
in other colonies.

The two years of Penn's first visit were probably

the happiest of his life. Always fond of the country, he built himself a fine seat on the Delaware
near Bristol, and it would have been better for
him, and probably also for the colony, if he had
remained there. But he thought he had duties
in England: his family needed him; he must de-
fend his people from the religious oppression still
prevailing; and Lord Baltimore had gone to England to resist him in the boundary dispute. One
of the more narrow-minded of his faith wrote to
Penn from England that he was enjoying himself
too much in his colony and seeking his own selfish
interest. Influenced by all these considerations,
he returned in August, 1684, and it was long before
he saw Pennsylvania again — not, indeed, until
October, 1699, and then for only two years.

CHAPTER III

LIFE IN PHILADELPHIA

THE rapid increase of population and the growing prosperity in Pennsylvania during the life of its founder present a striking contrast to the slower and more troubled growth of the other British colonies in America. The settlers in Pennsylvania engaged at once in profitable agriculture. The loam, clay, and limestone soils on the Pennsylvania side of the Delaware produced heavy crops of grain, as well as pasture for cattle and valuable lumber from its forests. The Pennsylvania settlers were of a class particularly skilled in dealing with the soil. They apparently encountered none of the difficulties, due probably to incompetent farming, which beset the settlers of Delaware, whose land was as good as that of the Pennsylvania colonists.

In a few years the port of Philadelphia was loading abundant cargoes for England and the great West India trade. After much experimenting

with different places on the river, such as New
Castle, Wilmington, Salem, Burlington, the Quakers had at last found the right location for a great
seat of commerce and trade that could serve as
a center for the export of everything from the region behind it and around it. Philadelphia thus
soon became the basis of a prosperity which no
other townsite on the Delaware had been able to
attain. The Quakers of Philadelphia were the
soundest of financiers and men of business, and
in their skillful hands the natural resources of their
colony were developed without setback or accident. At an early date banking institutions were
established in Philadelphia, and the strongest colonial merchants and mercantile firms had their
offices there. It was out of such a sound business
life that were produced in Revolutionary times
such characters as Robert Morris and after the
Revolution men like Stephen Girard.

Pennsylvania in colonial times was ruled from
Philadelphia somewhat as France has always been
ruled from Paris. And yet there was a difference:
Pennsylvania had free government. The Germans and the Scotch-Irish outnumbered the Quakers and could have controlled the Legislature,
for in 1750 out of a population of 150,000 the

Quakers were only about 50,000; and yet the
Legislature down to the Revolution was always
confided to the competent hands of the Quakers.
No higher tribute, indeed, has ever been paid to any
group of people as governors of a commonwealth
and architects of its finance and trade.

It is a curious commentary on the times and on
human nature that these Quaker folk, treated as
outcasts and enemies of good order and religion
in England and gradually losing all their property
in heavy fines and confiscations, should so suddenly in the wilderness prove the capacity of their
"Holy Experiment" for achieving the best sort
of good order and material success. They immediately built a most charming little town by the
waterside, snug and pretty with its red brick
houses in the best architectural style. It was
essentially a commercial town down to the time
of the Revolution and long afterwards. The
principal residences were on Water Street, the
second street from the wharves. The town in
those days extended back only as far as Fourth
Street, and the State House, now Independence
Hall, an admirable instance of the local brick
architecture, stood on the edge of the town. The
Pennsylvania Hospital the first institution of its

kind to be built in America, was situated out in the fields.

Through the town ran a stream following the line of the present Dock Street. Its mouth had been a natural landing place for the first explorers and for the Indians from time immemorial. Here stood a neat tavern, the Blue Anchor, with its dovecotes in old English style, looking out for many a year over the river with its fleet of small boats. Along the wharves lay the very solid, broad, somber, Quaker-like brick warehouses, some of which have survived into modern times. Everywhere were to be found ships and the good seafaring smell of tar and hemp. Ships were built and fitted out alongside docks where other ships were lading. A privateer would receive her equipment of guns, pistols, and cutlasses on one side of a wharf, while on the other side a ship was peacefully loading wheat or salted provisions for the West Indies.

Everybody's attention in those days was centered on the water instead of inland on railroads as it is today. Commerce was the source of wealth of the town as agriculture was the wealth of the interior of the province. Every one lived close to the river and had an interest in the rise and fall of the tide. The little town extended for a mile along the water but scarcely half a mile back from it. All communication with other places, all news from the world of Europe came from the ships, whose captains brought the letters and the few newspapers which reached the colonists. An important ship on her arrival often fired a gun and dropped anchor with some ceremony. Immediately the shore boats swarmed to her side; the captain was besieged for news and usually brought the letters ashore to be distributed at the coffeehouse. This institution took the place of the modern stock exchange, clearing house, newspaper, university, club, and theater all under one roof, with plenty to eat and drink besides. Within its rooms vessels and cargoes were sold; before its door negro slaves were auctioned off; and around it as a common center were brought together all sorts of business, valuable information, gossip, and scandal. It must have been a brilliant scene in the evening, with the candles lighting embroidered red and yellow waistcoats, blue and scarlet coats, green and black velvet, with the rich drab and mouse color of the prosperous Quakers contrasting with the uniforms of British officers come to fight the French and Indian wars.

Sound, as well as color, had its place in this busy and happy colonial life. Christ Church, a brick building which still stands the perfection of colonial architecture had been established by the Church of England people defiantly in the midst of heretical Quakerdom. It soon possessed a chime of bells sent out from England. Captain Budden, who brought them in his ship *Myrtilla,* would charge no freight for so charitable a deed, and in consequence of his generosity every time he and his ship appeared in the harbor the bells were rung in his honor. They were rung on market days to please the farmers who came into town with their wagons loaded with poultry and vegetables. They were rung muffled in times of public disaster and were kept busy in that way in the French and Indian wars. They were also rung muffled for Franklin when it was learned that while in London he had favored the Stamp Act — a means of expressing popular opinion which the newspapers subsequently put out of date.

The severe Quaker code of conduct and peaceful contemplation contains no prohibition against good eating and drinking. Quakers have been known to have the gout. The opportunities in Philadelphia to enjoy the pleasures of the table were soon unlimited. Farm, garden, and dairy products, vegetables, poultry, beef, and mutton were soon produced in immense quantity and variety and of excellent quality. John Adams, coming from the "plain living and high thinking" of Boston to attend the first meeting of the Continental Congress in Philadelphia, was invited to dine with Stephen Collins, a typical Quaker, and was amazed at the feast set before him. From that time his diary records one after another of these "sinful feasts," as he calls them. But the sin at which he thus looks askance never seems to have withheld him from a generous indulgence. "Drank Madeira at a great rate," he says on one occasion, "and took no harm from it." Madeira obtained in the trade with Spain was the popular drink even at the taverns. Various forms of punch and rum were common, but the modern light wines and champagne were not then in vogue.

Food in great quantity and variety seems to have been placed on the table at the same time, with little regard to formal courses. Beef, poultry, and mutton would all be served at one dinner. Fruit and nuts were placed on the table in profusion, as well as puddings and desserts numerous and deadly. Dinners were served usually in the afternoon. The splendid banquet which Adams describes as given to some members of the Continental Congress by Chief Justice Chew at his country seat was held at four in the afternoon. The dinner hour was still in the afternoon long after the Revolution and down to the times of the Civil War.

Other relics of this old love of good living lasted into modern times. It was not so very long ago that an occasional householder of wealth and distinction in Philadelphia could still be found who insisted on doing his own marketing in the old way, going himself the first thing in the morning on certain days to the excellent markets and purchasing all the family supplies. Philadelphia poultry is still famous the country over; and to be a good judge of poultry was in the old days as much a point of merit as to be a good judge of Madeira. A typical Philadelphian, envious New Yorkers say, will still keep a line of depositors waiting at a bank while he discourses to the receiving teller on what a splendid purchase of poultry he had made that morning. Early in the last century a wealthy leader of the bar is said to have continued the old practice of going to market followed by a negro with a wheelbarrow to bring back the supplies.

Not content with feasting in their own homes, the colonial Philadelphians were continually banqueting at the numerous taverns, from the Coach and Horses, opposite the State House, down to the Penny Pot Inn close by the river. At the Coach and Horses, where the city elections were usually held, the discarded oyster shells around it had been trampled into a hard white and smooth floor over which surged the excited election crowds. In those taverns the old fashion prevailed of roasting great joints of meat on a turnspit before an open fire; and to keep the spit turning before the heat little dogs were trained to work in a sort of treadmill cage.

In nothing is this colonial prosperity better revealed than in the quality of the country seats. They were usually built of stone and sometimes of brick and stone, substantial, beautifully proportioned, admirable in taste, with a certain simplicity, yet indicating a people of wealth, leisure, and refinement, who believed in themselves and took pleasure in adorning their lives. Not a few of these homes on the outskirts of the city have come down to us unharmed, and Cliveden, Stenton, and Belmont are precious relics of such solid structure that with ordinary care they will still last for centuries. Many were destroyed during the Revolution; others, such as Landsdowne, the seat of one of the Penn family, built in the Italian style, have disappeared; others were wiped out by the city's growth. All of them, even the small ones, were most interesting and typical of the life of the times. The colonists began to build them very early. A family would have a solid, brick town house and, only a mile or so away, a country house which was equally substantial. Sometimes they built at a greater distance. Governor Keith, for example, had a country seat, still standing though built in the middle of the eighteenth century, some twenty-five miles north of the city in what was then almost a wilderness.

Penn's ideal had always been to have Philadelphia what he called "a green country town." Probably he had in mind the beautiful English towns of abundant foliage and open spaces. And Penn was successful, for many of the Philadelphia houses stood by themselves, with gardens round them. The present Walnut was first called Pool Street; Chestnut was called Winn Street; and Market was called High Street. If he could have foreseen the enormous modern growth of the city, he might not have made his streets so narrow and level. But the fault lies perhaps rather with the people for adhering so rigidly and for so long to Penn's scheme, when traffic that he could not have imagined demanded wider streets. If he could have lived into our times he would surely have sent us very positive directions in his bluff British way to break up the original rectangular, narrow plan which was becoming dismally monotonous when applied to a widely spread-out modern city. He was a theologian, but he had a very keen eye for appearances and beauty of surroundings.

CHAPTER IV

TYPES OF THE POPULATION

The arrival of colonists in Pennsylvania in greater numbers than in Delaware and the Jerseys was the more notable because, within a few years after Pennsylvania was founded, persecution of the Quakers ceased in England and one prolific cause of their migration was no more. Thirteen hundred Quakers were released from prison in 1686 by James II; and in 1689, when William of Orange took the throne, toleration was extended to the Quakers and other Protestant dissenters.

The success of the first Quakers who came to America brought others even after persecution ceased in England. The most numerous class of immigrants for the first fifteen or twenty years were Welsh, most of whom were Quakers with a few Baptists and Church of England people. They may have come not so much from a desire to flee from persecution as to build up a little

Welsh community and to revive Welsh national-
ism. In their new surroundings they spoke their
own Welsh language and very few of them had
learned English. They had been encouraged in
their national aspirations by an agreement with
Penn that they were to have a tract of 40,000 acres
where they could live by themselves. The land
assigned to them lay west of Philadelphia in that
high ridge along the present main line of the Pennsylvania Railroad, now so noted for its wealthy
suburban homes. All the important names of
townships and places in that region, such as Wynne-
wood, St. Davids, Berwyn, Bryn Mawr, Merion,
Haverford, Radnor, are Welsh in origin. Some
of the Welsh spread round to the north of Philadelphia, where names like Gwynedd and Penllyn
remain as their memorials. The Chester Valley
bordering the high ridge of their first settlement
they called Duffrin Mawr or Great Valley.

These Welsh, like so many of the Quakers, were
of a well-to-do class. They rapidly developed
their fertile land and, for pioneers, lived quite
luxuriously. They had none of the usual county
and township officers but ruled their Welsh Barony,
as it was called, through the authority of their
Quaker meetings. But this system eventually

disappeared. The Welsh were absorbed into the English population, and in a couple of generations their language disappeared. Prominent people are descended from them. David Rittenhouse, the astronomer, was Welsh on his mother's side. David Lloyd, for a long time the leader of the popular party and at one time Chief Justice, was a Welshman. Since the Revolution the Welsh names of Cadwalader and Meredith have been conspicuous.

The Church of England people formed a curious and decidedly hostile element in the early population of Pennsylvania. They established themselves in Philadelphia in the beginning and rapidly grew into a political party which, while it cannot be called very strong in numbers, was important in ability and influence. After Penn's death, his sons joined the Church of England, and the Churchmen in the province became still stronger. They formed the basis of the proprietary party, filled executive offices in the Government, and waged relentless war against the Quaker majority which controlled the Legislature. During Penn's lifetime the Churchmen were naturally opposed to the whole government, both executive and legislative. They were constantly sending home to

England all sorts of reports and information cal-
culated to show that the Quakers were unfit to
rule a province, that Penn should be deprived of
his charter, and that Pennsylvania should be put
under the direct rule of the King.

They had delightful schemes for making it a
strong Church of England colony like Virginia.
One of them suggested that, as the title to the
Three Lower Counties, as Delaware was called,
was in dispute, it should be taken by the Crown
and given to the Church as a manor to support a
bishop. Such an ecclesiastic certainly could have
lived in princely state from the rents of its fertile
farms, with a palace, retinue, chamberlains, chan-
cellors, feudal courts, and all the appendages of
earthly glory. For the sake of the picturesqueness of colonial history it is perhaps a pity that
this pious plan was never carried out.

As it was, however, the Churchmen established
themselves with not a little glamour and romance
round two institutions, Christ Church for the first
fifty years, and after that round the old College
of Philadelphia. The Reverend William Smith, a
pugnacious and eloquent Scotchman, led them in
many a gallant onset against the "haughty tribe"
of Quakers, and he even suffered imprisonment in

the cause. He had a country seat on the Schuylkill and was in his way a fine character, devoted
to the establishment of ecclesiasticism and higher learning as a bulwark against the menace of
Quaker fanaticism; and but for the coming on of
the Revolution he might have become the first
colonial bishop with all the palaces, pomp, and glory
appertaining thereunto.

In spite of this opposition, however, the Quakers continued their control of the colony, serenely
tolerating the anathemas of the learned Churchmen and the fierce curses and brandished weapons
of the Presbyterians and Scotch-Irish. Curses
and anathemas were no check to the fertile soil.
Grist continued to come to the mill; and the agricultural products poured into Philadelphia to be
carried away in the ships. The contemplative
Quaker took his profits as they passed; enacted
his liberalizing laws, his prison reform, his charities, his peace with the savage Indians; allowed
science, research, and all the kindly arts of life to
flourish; and seemed perfectly contented with the
damnation in the other world to which those who
flourished under his rule consigned him.

In discussing the remarkable success of the
province, the colonists always disputed whether

the credit should be given to the fertile soil or to the liberal laws and constitution. It was no doubt due to both. But the obvious advantages of Penn's charter over the mixed and troublesome governmental conditions in the Jerseys, Penn's personal fame and the repute of the Quakers for liberalism then at its zenith, and the wide advertising given to their ideas and Penn's, on the continent of Europe as well as in England, seem to have been the reasons why more people, and many besides Quakers, came to take advantage of that fertile soil.

The first great increase of alien population came from Germany, which was still in a state of religious turmoil, disunion, and depression from the results of the Reformation and the Thirty Years' War. The reaction from dogma in Germany had produced a multitude of sects, all yearning for greater liberty and prosperity than they had at home. Penn and other Quakers had made missionary tours in Germany and had preached to the people. The Germans do not appear to have been asked to come to the Jerseys. But they were urged to come to Pennsylvania as soon as the charter was obtained; and many of them made an immediate response.

The German mind was then at the height of its emotional unrestraint. It was as unaccustomed to liberty of thought as to political liberty and it produced a new sect or religious distinction almost every day. Many of these sects came to Pennsylvania, where new small religious bodies sprang up among them after their arrival. Schwenkfelders, Tunkers, Labadists, New Born, New Mooners, Separatists, Zion's Brueder, Ronsdorfer, Inspired, Quietists, Gichtelians, Depellians, Mountain Men, River Brethren, Brinser Brethren, and the Society of the Woman in the Wilderness, are names which occur in the annals of the province. But these are only a few. In Lancaster County alone the number has at different times been estimated at from twenty to thirty. It would probably be impossible to make a complete list; some of them, indeed, existed for only a few years. Their own writers describe them as countless and bewildering. Many of them were characterized by the strangest sort of German mysticism, and some of them were inclined to monastic and hermit life and their devotees often lived in caves or solitary huts in the woods.

It would hardly be accurate to call all the German sects Quakers, since a great deal of their mysticism would have been anything but congenial to the followers of Fox and Penn. Resemblances to Quaker doctrine can, however, be found among many of them; and there was one large sect, the Mennonites, who were often spoken of as German Quakers. The two divisions fraternized and preached in each other's meetings. The Mennonites were well educated as a class and Pastorius, their leader, was a ponderously learned German. Most of the German sects left the Quakers in undisturbed possession of Philadelphia, and spread out into the surrounding region, which was then a wilderness. They and all the other Germans who afterwards followed them settled in a half circle beginning at Easton on the Delaware, passing up the Lehigh Valley into Lancaster County, thence across the Susquehanna and down the Cumberland Valley to the Maryland border, which many of them crossed, and in time scattered far to the south in Virginia and even North Carolina, where their descendants are still found.

These German sects which came over under the influence of Penn and the Quakers, between the years 1682 and 1702, formed a class by themselves. Though they may be regarded as peculiar in their ideas and often in their manner of life, it cannot be denied that as a class they were a well-educated, thrifty, and excellent people and far superior to the rough German peasants who followed them in later years. This latter class was often spoken of in Pennsylvania as "the church people," to distinguish them from "the sects," as those of the earlier migration were called.

The church people, or peasantry of the later migration, belonged usually to one of the two dominant churches of Germany, the Lutheran or the Reformed. Those of the Reformed Church were often spoken of as Calvinists. This migration of the church people was not due to the example of the Quakers but was the result of a new policy which was adopted by the British Government when Queen Anne ascended the throne in 1702, and which aimed at keeping the English people at home and at filling the English colonies in America with foreign Protestants hostile to France and Spain.

Large numbers of these immigrants were "redemptioners," as they were called; that is to say, they were persons who had been obliged to sell themselves to the shipping agents to pay for their passage. On their arrival in Pennsylvania the captain sold them to the colonists to pay the passage, and the redemptioner had to work for his owner for a period varying from five to ten years. No stigma or disgrace clung to any of these people under this system. It was regarded as a necessary business transaction. Not a few of the very respectable families of the State and some of its prominent men are known to be descended from redemptioners.

This method of transporting colonists proved a profitable trade for the shipping people, and was soon regularly organized like the modern assisted immigration. Agents, called "newlanders" and "soul-sellers," traveled through Germany working up the transatlantic traffic by various devices, some of them not altogether creditable. Pennsylvania proved to be the most attractive region for these immigrants. Some of those who were taken to other colonies finally worked their way to Pennsylvania. Practically none went to New England, and very few, if any, to Virginia. Indeed, only certain colonies were willing to admit them.

Another important element that went to make up the Pennsylvania population consisted of the Scotch-Irish. They were descendants of Scotch and English Presbyterians who had gone to Ireland to take up the estates of the Irish rebels confiscated under Queen Elizabeth and James I. This migration of Protestants to Ireland, which began soon after 1600, was encouraged by the English Government. Towards the middle of the seventeenth century the confiscation of more Irish land under Cromwell's régime increased the migration to Ulster. Many English joined the migration, and Scotch of the Lowlands who were largely of English extraction, although there were many Gaelic or Celtic names among them.

These are the people usually known in English history as Ulstermen — the same who made such a heroic defense of Londonderry against James II, and the same who in modern times have resisted home rule in Ireland because it would bury them, they believe, under the tyranny of their old enemies, the native Irish Catholic majority. They were more thrifty and industrious than the native Irish and as a result they usually prospered on the Irish land. At first they were in a more or less constant state of war with the native Irish, who attempted to expel them. They were subsequently persecuted by the Church of England under Charles I, who attempted to force them to conform to the English established religion. Such a rugged schooling in Ireland made of them a very

aggressive, hardy people, Protestants of the Protestants, so accustomed to contests and warfare
that they accepted it as the natural state of man.

These Ulstermen came to Pennsylvania somewhat later than the first German sects; and not
many of them arrived until some years after 1700.
They were not, like the first Germans, attracted
to the colony by any resemblance of their religion
to that of the Quakers. On the contrary they
were entirely out of sympathy with the Quakers,
except in the one point of religious liberty; and
the Quakers were certainly out of sympathy with
them. Nearly all the colonies in America received
a share of these settlers. Wherever they went
they usually sought the frontier and the wilderness; and by the time of the Revolution, they
could be found upon the whole colonial frontier
from New Hampshire to Georgia. They were
quite numerous in Virginia, and most numerous
along the edge of the Pennsylvania wilderness. It
was apparently the liberal laws and the fertile soil
that drew them to Pennsylvania in spite of their
contempt for most of the Quaker doctrines.

The dream of their life, their haven of rest, was
for these Scotch-Irish a fertile soil where they
would find neither Irish "papists" nor Church of

England; and for this reason in America they always sought the frontier where they could be by themselves. They could not even get on well with the Germans in Pennsylvania; and when the Germans crowded into their frontier settlements, quarrels became so frequent that the proprietors asked the Ulstermen to move farther west, a suggestion which they were usually quite willing to accept. At the close of the colonial period in Pennsylvania the Quakers, the Church of England people, and the miscellaneous denominations occupied Philadelphia and the region round it in a half circle from the Delaware River. Outside of this area lay another containing the Germans, and beyond that were the Scotch-Irish. The principal stronghold of the Scotch-Irish was the Cumberland Valley in Southern Pennsylvania west of the Susquehanna, a region now containing the flourishing towns of Chambersburg, Gettysburg, Carlisle, and York, where the descendants of these early settlers are still very numerous. In modern times, however, they have spread out widely; they are now to be found all over the State, and they no longer desire so strongly to live by themselves.

The Ulstermen, owing to the circumstances of

their earlier life, had no sympathy whatever with the Quaker's objection to war or with his desire to deal fairly with the Indians and pay them for their land. As Presbyterians and Calvinists, they belonged to one of the older and more conservative divisions of the Reformation. The Quaker's doctrine of the inward light, his quietism, contemplation, and advanced ideas were quite incomprehensible to them. As for the Indians, they held that the Old Testament commands the destruction of all the heathen; and as for paying the savages for their land, it seemed ridiculous to waste money on such an object when they could exterminate the natives at less cost. The Ulstermen, therefore, settled on the Indian land as they pleased, or for that matter on any land, and were continually getting into difficulty with the Pennsylvania Government no less than with the Indians. They regarded any region into which they entered as constituting a sovereign state. It was this feeling of independence which subsequently prompted them to organize what is known as the Whisky Rebellion when, after the Revolution, the Federal Government put a tax on the liquor which they so much esteemed as a product, for corn converted into whisky was more easily transported on horses

over mountain trails, and in that form fetched a
better price in the markets.

After the year 1755, when the Quaker method
of dealing with the Indians no longer prevailed,
the Scotch-Irish lived on the frontier in a contin-
ual state of savage warfare which lasted for the
next forty years. War, hunting the abundant
game, the deer, buffalo, and elk, and some agriculture filled the measure of their days and years.
They paid little attention to the laws of the province, which were difficult to enforce on the distant
frontier, and they administered a criminal code of
their own with whipping or "laced jacket," as
they called it, as a punishment. They were Jacks
of all trades, weaving their own cloth and making
nearly everything they needed. They were the
first people in America to develop the use of the
rifle, and they used it in the Back Country all the
way down into the Carolinas at a time when it
was seldom seen in the seaboard settlements. In
those days, rifles were largely manufactured in
Lancaster, Pennsylvania, and there were several
famous gunsmiths in Philadelphia. Some of the
best of these old rifles have been preserved and
are really beautiful weapons, with delicate hair
triggers, gracefully curved stocks, and quaint brass

or even gold or silver mountings.   The ornamentation was often done by the hunter himself, who would melt a gold or silver coin and pour it into some design which he had carved with his knife in the stock.

The Revolution offered an opportunity after the Ulstermen's heart, and they entered it with their entire spirit, as they had every other contest which involved liberty and independence.   In fact, in that period they played such a conspicuous part that they almost ruled Philadelphia, the original home of the Quakers.   Since then, spread out through the State, they have always had great influence, the natural result of their energy, intelligence, and love of education.

Nearly all these diverse elements of the Pennsylvania population were decidedly sectional in character.   The Welsh had a language of their own, and they attempted, though without success, to maintain it, as well as a government of their own within their barony independent of the regular government of the province.   The Germans were also extremely sectional.   They clung with better success to their own language, customs, and literature.   The Scotch-Irish were so clannish that they had ideas of founding a separate province on

the Susquehanna. Even the Church of England
people were so aloof and partisan that, though
they lived about Philadelphia among the Quakers,
they were extremely hostile to the Quaker rule and
unremittingly strove to destroy it.

All these cleavages and divisions in the population continue in their effects to this day. They
prevented the development of a homogeneous
population. No exact statistics were taken of
the numbers of the different nationalities in colonial times; but Franklin's estimate is probably
fairly accurate, and his position in practical politics gave him the means of knowing and of testing
his calculations. About the year 1750 he estimated the population as one-third Quaker, one-
third German, and one-third miscellaneous. This
gave about 50,000 or 60,000 to each of the thirds.
Provost Smith, of the newly founded college, estimated the Quakers at only about 40,000. But
his estimate seems too low. He was interested in
making out their numbers small because he was
trying to show the absurdity of allowing such a
small band of fanatics and heretics to rule a great
province of the British Empire. One great source
of the Quaker power lay in the sympathy of the
Germans, who always voted on their side and kept

them in control of the Legislature, so that it was in reality a case of two-thirds ruling one-third. The Quakers, it must be admitted, never lost their heads. Unperturbed through all the conflicts and the jarring of races and sects, they held their position unimpaired and kept the confidence and support of the Germans until the Revolution changed everything.

The varied elements of population spread out in ever widening half circles from Philadelphia as a center. There was nothing in the character of the region to stop this progress. The country all the way westward to the Susquehanna was easy hill, dale, and valley, covered by a magnificent growth of large forest trees — oaks, beeches, poplars, walnuts, hickories, and ash — which rewarded the labor of felling by exposing to cultivation a most fruitful soil.

The settlers followed the old Indian trails. The first westward pioneers seem to have been the Welsh Quakers, who pushed due west from Philadelphia and marked out the course of the famous Lancaster Road, afterwards the Lancaster Turnpike. It took the line of least resistance along the old trail, following ridges until it reached the Susquehanna at a spot where an Indian trader,

named Harris, established himself and founded a
post which subsequently became Harrisburg, the
capital of the State.

For a hundred years the Lancaster Road was
the great highway westward, at first to the mountains, then to the Ohio, and finally to the Mississippi Valley and the Great West. Immigrants
and pioneers from all the New England and Middle
States flocked out that way to the land of promise
in wagons, or horseback, or trudging along on foot.
Substantial taverns grew up along the route; and
habitual freighters and stage drivers, proud of
their fine teams of horses, grew into characters of
the road. When the Pennsylvania Railroad was
built, it followed the same line. In fact, most of
the lines of railroad in the State follow Indian trails.
The trails for trade and tribal intercourse led east
and west. The warrior trails usually led north
and south, for that had long been the line of
strategy and conquest of the tribes. The northern tribes, or Six Nations, established in the lake
region of New York near the headwaters of the
Delaware, the Susquehanna, and the Ohio, had the
advantage of these river valleys for descending into
the whole Atlantic seaboard and the valley of the
Mississippi. They had in consequence conquered

all the tribes south of them as far even as the Carolinas and Georgia. All their trails of conquest led across Pennsylvania.

The Germans in their expansion at first seem to have followed up the Schuylkill Valley and its tributaries, and they hold this region to the present day. Gradually they crossed the watershed to the Susquehanna and broke into the region of the famous limestone soil in Lancaster County, a veritable farmer's paradise from which nothing will ever drive them. Many Quaker farmers penetrated north and northeast from Philadelphia into Bucks County, a fine rolling and hilly wheat and corn region, where their descendants are still found and whence not a few well-known Philadelphia families have come.

The Quaker government of Pennsylvania in almost a century of its existence largely fulfilled its ideals. It did not succeed in governing without war; but the war was not its fault. It did succeed in governing without oaths. An affirmation instead of an oath became the law of Pennsylvania for all who chose an affirmation; and this law was soon adopted by most American communities. It succeeded in establishing religious liberty in Pennsylvania in the fullest sense of the word. It brought Christianity nearer to its original simplicity and made it less superstitious and cruel.

The Quakers had always maintained that it was a mistake to suppose that their ideas would interfere with material prosperity and happiness; and they certainly proved their contention in Pennsylvania. To Quaker liberalism was due not merely the material prosperity, but prison reform and the notable public charities of Pennsylvania; in both of which activities, as in the abolition of slavery, the Quakers were leaders. Original research in science also flourished in a marked degree in colonial Pennsylvania. No one in those days knew the nature of thunder and lightning, and the old explanation that they were the voice of an angry God was for many a sufficient explanation. Franklin, by a long series of experiments in the free Quaker colony, finally proved in 1752 that lightning was electricity, that is to say, a manifestation of the same force that is produced when glass is rubbed with buckskin. He invented the lightning rod, discovered the phenomenon of positive and negative electricity, explained the action of the Leyden jar, and was the first American writer on the modern science of political economy. This energetic citizen of Pennsylvania spent a large part of his life in research; he studied the Gulf Stream, storms and their causes, waterspouts, whirlwinds; and he established the fact that the northeast storms of the Atlantic coast usually move against the wind.

But Franklin was not the only scientist in the colony. Besides his three friends, Kinnersley, Hopkinson, and Syng, who worked with him and helped him in his discoveries, there were David Rittenhouse, the astronomer, John Bartram, the botanist, and a host of others. Rittenhouse excelled in every undertaking which required the practical application of astronomy, He attracted attention even in Europe for his orrery which indicated the movements of the stars and which was an advance on all previous instruments of the kind. When astronomers in Europe were seeking to have the transit of Venus of 1769 observed in different parts of the world, Pennsylvania alone of the American colonies seems to have had the man and the apparatus necessary for the work. Rittenhouse conducted the observations at three points and won a world-wide reputation by the accuracy and skill of his observations. The whole community was interested in this scientific undertaking; the Legislature and public institutions raised the necessary funds; and the American Philosophical Society, the only organization of its kind in the colonies, had charge of the preparations.

The American Philosophical Society had been started in Philadelphia in 1743. It was the first scientific society to be founded in America, and throughout the colonial period it was the only society of its kind in the country. Its membership included not only prominent men throughout America, such as Thomas Jefferson, who were interested in scientific inquiry, but also representatives of foreign nations. With its library of rare and valuable collections and its annual publication of essays on almost every branch of science, the society still continues its useful scientific work.

John Bartram, who was the first botanist to describe the plants of the New World and who explored the whole country from the Great Lakes to Florida, was a Pennsylvania Quaker of colonial times, farmer born and bred. Thomas Godfrey, also a colonial Pennsylvanian, was rewarded by the Royal Society of England for an improvement which he made in the quadrant. Peter Collinson of England, a famous naturalist and antiquarian of early times, was a Quaker. In modern times

John Dalton, the discoverer of the atomic theory and of color-blindness, was born of Quaker parents, and Edward Cope, of a well-known Philadelphia Quaker family, became one of the most eminent naturalists and paleontologists of the nineteenth century, and unaided discovered over a third of the three thousand extinct species of vertebrates recognized by men of science. In the field of education, Lindley Murray, the grammarian of a hundred years ago, was a Quaker. Ezra Cornell, a Quaker, founded the great university in New York which bears his name; and Johns Hopkins, also a Quaker, founded the university of that name in Baltimore.

Pennsylvania deserves the credit of turning these early scientific pursuits to popular uses. The first American professorship of botany and natural history was established in Philadelphia College, now the University of Pennsylvania. The first American book on a medical subject was written in Philadelphia by Thomas Cadwalader in 1740; the first American hospital was established there in 1751; and the first systematic instruction in medicine. Since then Philadelphia has produced a long line of physicians and surgeons of national and European reputation. For half a century after the Revolution the city was the center of medical education for the country and it still retains a large part of that preëminence. The Academy of Natural Sciences founded in Philadelphia in 1812 by two inconspicuous young men, an apothecary and a dentist, soon became by the spontaneous support of the community a distinguished institution. It sent out two Arctic expeditions, that of Kane and that of Hayes, and has included among its members the most prominent men of science in America. It is now the oldest as well as the most complete institution of its kind in the country. The Franklin Institute, founded in Philadelphia in 1824, was the result of a similar scientific interest. It was the first institution of applied science and the mechanic arts in America. Descriptions of the first 2900 patents issued by the United States Government are to be found only on the pages of its *Journal*, which is still an authoritative annual record.

Apart from their scientific attainments, one of the most interesting facts about the Quakers is the large proportion of them who have reached eminence, often in occupations which are supposed to be somewhat inconsistent with Quaker doctrine. General Greene, the most capable American officer of the Revolution, after Washington, was a Rhode

Island Quaker. General Mifflin of the Revolution was a Pennsylvania Quaker. General Jacob Brown, a Bucks County Pennsylvania Quaker, reorganized the army in the War of 1812 and restored it to its former efficiency. In the long list of Quakers eminent in all walks of life, not only in Pennsylvania but elsewhere, are to be found John Bright, a lover of peace and human liberty through a long and eminent career in British politics; John Dickinson of Philadelphia, who wrote the famous *Farmer's Letters* so signally useful in the American Revolution; Whittier, the American poet, a Quaker born in Massachusetts of a family converted from Puritanism when the Quakers invaded Boston in the seventeenth century; and Benjamin West, a Pennsylvania Quaker of colonial times, an artist of permanent eminence, one of the founders of the Royal Academy in England and its president in succession to Sir Joshua Reynolds.

Wherever Quakers are found they are the useful and steady citizens. Their eminence seems out of all proportion to their comparatively small numbers. It has often been asked why this height of attainment should occur among a people of such narrow religious discipline. But were the Quakers really narrow, or were they any more narrow than other rigorously self-disciplined people — Spartans, Puritans, soldiers whose discipline enables them to achieve great results? All discipline is in one sense narrow. Quaker quietude and retirement probably conserved mental energy instead of dissipating it. In an age of superstition and irrational religion, their minds were free and unhampered, and it was the dominant rational tone of their thought that enabled science to flourish in Pennsylvania.

CHAPTER V

THE TROUBLES OF PENN AND HIS SONS

THE material prosperity of Penn's Holy Experiment kept on proving itself over and over again every month of the year. But meantime great events were taking place in England. The period of fifteen years from Penn's return to England in 1684, until his return to Pennsylvania at the close of the year of 1699, was an eventful time in English history. It was long for a proprietor to be away from his province, and Penn would have left a better reputation if he had passed those fifteen years in his colony, for in England during that period he took what most Americans believe to have been the wrong side in the Revolution of 1688.

Penn was closely tied by both interest and friendship to Charles II and the Stuart family. When Charles II died in 1685 and his brother, the Duke of York, ascended the throne as James II, Penn was equally bound to him, because among other things the Duke of York had obtained Penn's release in 1669 from imprisonment for his religious opinions. He became still more bound when one of the first acts of the new King's reign was the release of a great number of people who had been imprisoned for their religion, among them thirteen hundred Quakers. In addition to preaching to the Quakers and protecting them, Penn used his influence with James to secure the return of several political offenders from exile. His friendship with James raised him, indeed, to a position of no little importance at Court. He was constantly consulted by the King, in whose political policy he gradually became more and more involved.

James was a Roman Catholic and soon perfected his plans for making both Church and State a papal appendage and securing for the Crown the right to suspend acts of Parliament. Penn at first protested, but finally supported the King in the belief that he would in the end establish liberty. In his earlier years, however, Penn had written pamphlets arguing strenuously against the same sort of despotic schemes that James was now undertaking; and this contradiction of his former position seriously injured his reputation even among his own people.

Part of the policy of James was to grant many favors to the Quakers and to all other dissenting bodies in England, to release them from prison, to give them perfect freedom of worship, and to remove the test laws which prevented them from holding office. He thus hoped to unite them with the Roman Catholics in extirpating the Church of England and establishing the Papacy in its place. But the dissenters and nonconformists, though promised relief from sufferings severer than it is possible perhaps now to appreciate, refused almost to a man this tempting bait. Even the Quakers, who had suffered probably more than the others, rejected the offer with indignation and mourned the fatal mistake of their leader Penn. All Protestant England united in condemning him, accused him of being a secret Papist and a Jesuit in disguise, and believed him guilty of acts and intentions of which he was probably entirely innocent. This extreme feeling against Penn is reflected in Macaulay's *History of England*, which strongly espouses the Whig side; and in those vivid pages Penn is represented, and very unfairly, as nothing less than a scoundrel.

In spite of the attempts which James made to secure his position, the dissenters, the Church of

England, and Penn's own Quakers all joined
heart and soul in the Revolution of 1688, which
quickly dethroned the King, drove him from
England, and placed the Prince of Orange on the
throne as William III. Penn was now for many
years in a very unfortunate, if not dangerous,
position, and was continually suspected of plotting
to restore James. For three years he was in
hiding to escape arrest or worse, and he largely
lost the good will and affection of the Quakers.

Meantime since his departure from Pennsylvania in the summer of 1684 that province went
on increasing in population and in pioneer prosperity. But Penn's quitrents and money from sales
of land were far in arrears, and he had been and
still was at great expense in starting the colony
and in keeping up the plantation and country seat
he had established on the Delaware River above
Philadelphia. Troublesome political disputes also
arose. The Council of eighteen members which
he had authorized to act as governor in his absence neglected to send the new laws to him, slight-
ed his letters, and published laws in their own name
without mentioning him or the King. These irregularities were much exaggerated by enemies
of the Quakers in England. The Council was not

a popular body and was frequently at odds with the Assembly.

Penn thought he could improve the government by appointing five commissioners to act as governor instead of the whole Council. Thomas Lloyd, an excellent Quaker who had been President of the Council and who had done much to allay hard feeling, was fortunately the president of these commissioners. Penn instructed them to act as if he himself were present, and at the next meeting of the Assembly to annul all the laws and reënact only such as seemed proper. This course reminds us of the absolutism of his friend, King James, and, indeed, the date of these instructions (1686) is that when his intimacy with that bigoted monarch reached its highest point. Penn's theory of his power was that the frame or constitution of government he had given the province was a contract; that, the Council and Assembly having violated some of its provisions, it was annulled and he was free, at least for a time, to govern as he pleased. Fortunately his commissioners never attempted to carry out these instructions. There would have been a rebellion and some very unpleasant history if they had undertaken to enforce such oriental despotism in Pennsylvania.

The five commissioners with Thomas Lloyd at their head seem to have governed without seriously troublesome incidents for the short term of two years during which they were in power. But in 1687 Thomas Lloyd, becoming weary of directing them, asked to be relieved and is supposed to have advised Penn to appoint a single executive instead of commissioners. Penn accordingly appointed Captain John Blackwell, formerly an officer in Cromwell's army. Blackwell was not a Quaker but a "grave, sober, wise man," as Penn wrote to a friend, who would "bear down with a visible authority vice and faction." It was hoped that he would vigorously check all irregularities and bring Penn better returns from quitrents and sales of land.

But this new governor clashed almost at once with the Assembly, tried to make them pass a militia law, suggested that the province's trade to foreign countries was illegal, persecuted and arrested members of the Assembly, refused to submit new laws to it, and irritated the people by suggesting the invalidity of their favorite laws. The Quaker Assembly withstood and resisted him until they wore him out. After a year and one month in office he resigned at Penn's request or,

according to some accounts, at his own request.
At any rate, he expressed himself as delighted to
be relieved.   As a Puritan soldier he found himself no match for a peaceable Quaker Assembly.

Penn again made the Council the executive with
Thomas Lloyd as its President.   But to the old
causes of unrest a new one was now added.   One
George Keith, a Quaker, turned heretic and carried a number of Pennsylvania Quakers over to
the Church of England, thereby causing great
scandal.   The "Lower Counties" or Territories,
as the present State of Delaware was then called,
became mutinous, withdrew their representatives
from the Council, and made William Markham
their Governor.   This action together with the
Keithian controversy, the disturbances over Blackwell, and the clamors of Church of England people
that Penn was absent and neglecting his province,
that the Quakers would make no military defense,
and that the province might at any time fall into
the hands of France, came to the ears of King
William, who was already ill disposed toward
Penn and distrusted him as a Jacobite.   It seemed
hardly advisable to allow a Jacobite to rule a British colony.   Accordingly a royal order suspended
Penn's governmental authority and placed the

province under Benjamin Fletcher, Governor of New York. He undertook to rule in dictatorial fashion, threatening to annex the province to New York, and as a consequence the Assembly had plenty of trouble with him. But two years later, 1694, the province was returned to Penn, who now appointed as Governor William Markham, who had served as lieutenant-governor under Fletcher.

Markham proceeded to be high-handed with the Assembly and to administer the government in the imperialistic style of Fletcher. But the Assembly soon tamed him and in 1696 actually worried out of him a new constitution, which became known as Markham's Frame, proved much more popular than the one Penn had given, and allowed the Assembly much more power. Markham had no conceivable right to assent to it and Penn never agreed to it; but it was lived under for the next four years until Penn returned to the province. While it naturally had opponents, it was largely regarded as entirely valid, and apparently with the understanding that it was to last until Penn objected to it.

Penn had always been longing to return to Pennsylvania and live there for the rest of his life; but the terrible times of the Revolution of 1688 in England and its consequences had held him back. Those difficulties had now passed. Moreover, William III had established free government and religious liberty. No more Quakers were imprisoned and Penn's old occupation of securing their protection and release was gone.

In the autumn of 1699 he sailed for Pennsylvania with his family and, arriving after a tedious three months' voyage, was well received. His political scrapes and mistakes in England seemed to be buried in the past. He was soon at his old enjoyable life again, traveling actively about the country, preaching to the Quakers, and enlarging and beautifying his country seat, Pennsbury, on the Delaware, twenty miles above Philadelphia. As roads and trails were few and bad he usually traveled to and from the town in a barge which was rowed by six oarsmen and which seemed to give him great pride and pleasure.

Two happy years passed away in this manner, during which Penn seems to have settled, not however without difficulty, a great deal of business with his people, the Assembly, and the Indian tribes. Unfortunately he got word from England of a bill in Parliament for the revocation of colonial charters and for the establishment of royal governments in their place. He must needs return to England to fight it. Shortly before he sailed the Assembly presented him with a draft of a new constitution or frame of government which they had been discussing with him and preparing for some time. This he accepted, and it became the constitution under which Pennsylvania lived and prospered for seventy-five years, until the Revolution of 1776.

This new constitution was quite liberal. The most noticeable feature of it was the absence of any provision for the large elective council or upper house of legislation, which had been very unpopular. The Assembly thus became the one legislative body. There was incidental reference in the document to a governor's council, although there was no formal clause creating it. Penn and his heirs after his death always appointed a small council as an advisory body for the deputy governor. The Assembly was to be chosen annually by the freemen and to be composed of four representatives from each county. It could originate bills, control its own adjournments without interference from the Governor, choose its speaker and other officers, and judge of the qualifications and election of its own members. These were standard Anglo-Saxon popular parliamentary rights developed by long struggles in England and now established in Pennsylvania never to be relaxed. Finally a clause in the constitution permitted the Lower Counties, or Territories, under certain conditions to establish home rule. In 1705 the Territories took advantage of this concession and set up an assembly of their own.

Immediately after signing the constitution, in the last days of October, 1701, Penn sailed for England, expecting soon to return. But he became absorbed in affairs in England and never saw his colony again. This was unfortunate because Pennsylvania soon became a torment to him instead of a great pleasure as it always seems to have been when he lived in it. He was a happy present proprietor, but not a very happy absentee one.

The Church of England people in Pennsylvania entertained great hopes of this proposal to turn the proprietary colonies into royal provinces. Under such a change, while the Quakers might still have an influence in the Legislature, the Crown would probably give the executive offices to Churchmen. They therefore labored hard to discredit the Quakers. They kept harping on the absurdity of a set of fanatics attempting to govern a colony without a militia and without administering oaths of office or using oaths in judicial proceedings. How could any one's life be safe from foreign enemies without soldiers, and what safeguard was there for life, liberty, and property before judges, jurors, and witnesses, none of whom had been sworn? The Churchmen kept up their complaints for a long time, but without effect in England.

Penn was able to thwart all their plans. The bill to change the province into a royal one was never passed by Parliament. Penn returned to his court life, his preaching, and his theological writing, a rather curious combination and yet one by which he had always succeeded in protecting his people. He was a favorite with Queen Anne, who was now on the throne, and he led an expensive life which, with the cost of his deputy governor's salary in the colony, the slowness of his quit-rent collections, and the dishonesty of the steward of his English estates, rapidly brought him into debt. To pay the government expense of a small colonial empire and at the same time to lead the life of a courtier and to travel as a preacher would have exhausted a stronger exchequer than Penn's.

The contests between the different deputy governors, whom Penn or his descendants sent out, and the Quaker Legislature fill the annals of the province for the next seventy years, down to the Revolution. These quarrels, when compared with the larger national political contests of history, seem petty enough and even tedious in detail. But, looked at in another aspect, they are important because they disclose how liberty, self-government, republicanism, and many of the constitutional principles by which Americans now live were gradually developed as the colonies grew towards independence.

The keynote to all these early contests was what may be called the fundamental principle of colonial constitutional law or, at any rate, of constitutional practice, namely, that the Governor, whether royal or proprietary, must always be kept poor. His salary or income must never become a fixed or certain sum but must always be dependent on the annual favor and grants of a legislature controlled by the people. This belief was the foundation of American colonial liberty. The Assemblies, not only in Pennsylvania but in other colonies, would withhold the Governor's salary until he consented to their favorite laws. If he vetoed their laws, he received no salary. One of the causes of the Revolution in 1776 was the attempt of the mother country to make the governors and other colonial officials dependent for their salaries on the Government in England instead of on the legislatures in the colonies.

So the squabbles, as we of today are inclined to call them, went on in Pennsylvania — provincial and petty enough, but often very large and important so far as the principle which they involved was concerned. The Legislature of Pennsylvania in those days was a small body composed of only about twenty-five or thirty members, most of them sturdy, thrifty Quakers. They could meet very easily anywhere — at the Governor's house, if in conference with him, or at the treasurer's office or at the loan office, if investigating accounts. Beneath their broad brim hats and grave demeanor they were as Anglo-Saxon at heart as Robin Hood and his merry men, and in their ninety years of political control they built up as goodly a fabric of civil liberty as can be found in any community in the world.

The dignified, confident message from a deputy governor, full of lofty admonitions of their duty to the Crown, the province, and the proprietor,

is often met by a sarcastic, stinging reply of the
Assembly.   David Lloyd, the Welsh leader of the
anti-proprietary party, and Joseph Wilcox, another leader, became very skillful in drafting these
profoundly respectful but deeply cutting replies.
In after years, Benjamin Franklin attained even
greater skill.   In fact, it is not unlikely that he
developed a large measure of his world famous
aptness in the use of language in the process of
drafting these replies.   The composing of these
official communications was important work, for
a reply had to be telling and effective not only
with the Governor but with the people who learned
of its contents at the coffeehouse and spread the
report of it among all classes.   There was not a
little good-fellowship in their contests; and Franklin, for instance, tells us how he used to abuse a
certain deputy governor all day in the Assembly
and then dine with him in jovial intercourse in
the evening.

The Assembly had a very convenient way of
accomplishing its purposes in legislation in spite
of the opposition of the British Government.
Laws when passed and approved by the deputy
governor had to be sent to England for approval
by the Crown within five years.   But meanwhile

the people would live under the law for five years,
and, if at the end of that time it was disallowed,
the Assembly would reënact the measure and live
under it again for another period.

The ten years after Penn's return to England
in 1701 were full of trouble for him.   Money returns from the province were slow, partly because
England was involved in war and trade depressed,
and partly because the Assembly, exasperated by
the deputy governors he appointed, often refused
to vote the deputy a salary and left Penn to bear
all the expense of government.   He was being
rapidly overwhelmed with debt.   One of his sons
was turning out badly.   The manager of his estates in England and Ireland, Philip Ford, was en-
riching himself by the trust, charging compound
interest at eight per cent every six months, and
finally claiming that Penn owed him £14,000.
Ford had rendered accounts from time to time,
but Penn in his careless way had tossed them
aside without examination.   When Ford pressed
for payment, Penn, still without making any in-
vestigation, foolishly gave Ford a deed in fee
simple of Pennsylvania as security.   Afterwards
he accepted from Ford a lease of the province,

which was another piece of folly, for the lease could, of course, be used as evidence to show that the deed was an absolute conveyance and not intended as a mortgage.

This unfortunate business Ford kept quiet during his lifetime. But on his death his widow and son made everything public, professed to be the proprietors of Pennsylvania, and sued Penn for £2000 rent in arrears. They obtained a judgment for the amount claimed and, as Penn could not pay, they had him arrested and imprisoned for debt. For nine months he was locked up in the debtors' prison, the "Old Bailey," and there he might have remained indefinitely if some of his friends had not raised enough money to compromise with the Fords. Isaac Norris, a prominent Quaker from Pennsylvania, happened at that time to be in England and exerted himself to set Penn free and save the province from further disgrace. After this there was a reaction in Penn's favor. He selected a better deputy governor for Pennsylvania. He wrote a long and touching letter to the people, reminding them how they had flourished and grown rich and free under his liberal laws, while he had been sinking in poverty.

After that conditions improved in the affairs

of Penn. The colony was better governed, and the anti-proprietary party almost disappeared. The last six or eight years of Penn's life were free from trouble. He had ceased his active work at court, for everything that could be accomplished for the Quakers in the way of protection and favorable laws had now been done. Penn spent his last years in trying to sell the government of his province to the Crown for a sum that would enable him to pay his debts and to restore his family to prosperity. But he was too particular in stipulating that the great principles of civil and religious liberty on which the colony had been established should not be infringed. He had seen how much evil had resulted to the rights of the people when the proprietors of the Jerseys parted with their right to govern. In consequence he required so many safeguards that the sale of Pennsylvania was delayed and delayed until its founder was stricken with paralysis. Penn lingered for some years, but his intellect was now too much clouded to make a valid sale. The event, however, was fortunate for Pennsylvania, which would probably otherwise have lost many valuable rights and privileges by becoming a Crown colony.

On July 30, 1718, Penn died at the age of seventy-four. His widow became proprietor of the province, probably the only woman who ever became feudal proprietor of such an immense domain. She appointed excellent deputy governors and ruled with success for eight years until her death in 1726. In her time the ocean was free from enemy cruisers, and the trade of the colony grew so rapidly that the increasing sales of land and quitrents soon enabled her to pay off the mortgage on the province and all the rest of her husband's debts. It was sad that Penn did not live to see that day, which he had so hoped for in his last years, when, with ocean commerce free from depredations, the increasing money returns from his province would obviate all necessity of selling the government to the Crown.

With all debts paid and prosperity increasing, Penn's sons became very rich men. Death had reduced the children to three — John, Thomas, and Richard. Of these, Thomas became what may be called the managing proprietor, and the others were seldom heard of. Thomas lived in the colony nine years — 1732 to 1741 — studying its affairs and sitting as a member of the Council. For over forty years he was looked upon as the

proprietor. In fact, he directed the great province
for almost as long a time as his father had managed
it. But he was so totally unlike his father that it is
difficult to find the slightest resemblance in feature or in mind. He was not in the least disposed
to proclaim or argue about religion. Like the rest
of his family, he left the Quakers and joined the
Church of England, a natural evolution in the case
of many Quakers. He was a prosperous, accomplished, sensible, cool-headed gentleman, by no
means without ability, but without any inclination
for setting the world on fire. He was a careful,
economical man of business, which is more than
can be said of his distinguished father. He saw no
visions and cared nothing for grand speculations.

Thomas Penn, however, had his troubles and
disputes with the Assembly. They thought him
narrow and close. Perhaps he was. That was
the opinion of him held by Franklin, who led the
anti-proprietary party. But at the same time
some consideration must be given to the position
in which Penn found himself. He had on his
hands an empire, rich, fertile, and inhabited by
liberty-loving Anglo-Saxons and by passive Germans. He had to collect from their land the purchase money and quitrents rapidly rolling up in

value with the increase of population into millions of pounds sterling, for which he was responsible to his relatives. At the same time he had to influence the politics of the province, approve or reject laws in such a way that his family interest would be protected from attack or attempted confiscation, keep the British Crown satisfied, and see that the liberties of the colonists were not impaired and that the people were kept contented.

It was not an easy task even for a clear-headed man like Thomas Penn. He had to arrange for treaties with the Indians and for the purchase of their lands in accordance with the humane ideas of his father and in the face of the Scotch-Irish thirst for Indian blood and the French desire to turn the savages loose upon the Anglo-Saxon settlements. He had to fight through the boundary disputes with Connecticut, Maryland, and Virginia, which threatened to reduce his empire to a mere strip of land containing neither Philadelphia nor Pittsburgh. The controversy with Connecticut lasted throughout the colonial period and was not definitely settled till the close of the Revolution. The charter of Connecticut granted by the British Crown extended the colony westward to the Pacific Ocean and cut off the northern half of the tract afterwards granted to William Penn. In pursuance of what they believed to be their rights, the Connecticut people settled in the beautiful valley of Wyoming. They were thereupon ejected by force by the proprietors of Pennsylvania; but they returned, only to be ejected again and again in a petty warfare carried on for many years. In the summer of 1778, the people of the valley were massacred by the Iroquois Indians. The history of this Connecticut boundary dispute fills volumes. So does the boundary dispute with Maryland, which also lasted throughout the colonial period; the dispute with Virginia over the site of Pittsburgh is not so voluminous. All these controversies Thomas Penn conducted with eminent skill, inexhaustible patience, and complete success. For this achievement the State owes him a debt of gratitude.

Thomas Penn was in the extraordinary position of having to govern as a feudal lord what was virtually a modern community. He was exercising feudal powers three hundred years after all the reasons for the feudal system had ceased to exist; and he was exercising those powers and acquiring by them vast wealth from a people in a new and wild country whose convictions, both civil and religious, were entirely opposed to anything like the feudal system. It must certainly be put down as something to his credit that he succeeded so well as to retain control both of the political government and his family's increasing wealth down to the time of the Revolution and that he gave on the whole so little offense to a high-strung people that in the Revolution they allowed his family to retain a large part of their land and paid them liberally for what was confiscated.

The wealth which came to the three brothers they spent after the manner of the time in country life. John and Richard do not appear to have had remarkable country seats. But Thomas purchased in 1760 the fine English estate of Stoke Park, which had belonged to Sir Christopher Hatton of Queen Elizabeth's time, to Lord Coke, and later to the Cobham family. Thomas's son John, grandson of the founder, greatly enlarged and beautified the place and far down into the nineteenth century it was one of the notable country seats of England. This John Penn also built another country place called Pennsylvania Castle, equally picturesque and interesting, on the Isle of Portland, of which he was Governor.

CHAPTER VI

THE FRENCH AND INDIAN WAR

THERE was no great change in political conditions in Pennsylvania until about the year 1755. The French in Canada had been gradually developing their plans of spreading down the Ohio and Mississippi valleys behind the English colonies. They were at the same time securing alliances with the Indians and inciting them to hostilities against the English. But so rapidly were the settlers advancing that often the land could not be purchased fast enough to prevent irritation and ill feeling. The Scotch-Irish and Germans, it has already been noted, settled on lands without the formality of purchase from the Indians. The Government, when the Indians complained, sometimes ejected the settlers but more often hastened to purchase from the Indians the land which had been occupied. *The Importance of the British Plantations in America*, published in 1731, describes the Indians as peaceful and contented in Pennsylvania but irritated and unsettled in those other colonies where they had usually been illtreated and defrauded. This, with other evidence, goes to show that up to that time Penn's policy of fairness and good treatment still prevailed. But those conditions soon changed, as the famous Walking Purchase of 1737 clearly indicated.

The Walking Purchase had provided for the sale of some lands along the Delaware below the Lehigh on a line starting at Wrightstown, a few miles back from the Delaware not far above Trenton, and running northwest, parallel with the river, as far as a man could walk in a day and a half. The Indians understood that this tract would extend northward only to the Lehigh, which was the ordinary journey of a day and a half. The proprietors, however, surveyed the line beforehand, marked the trees, engaged the fastest walkers and, with horses to carry provisions, started their men at sunrise. By running a large part of the way, at the end of a day and a half these men had reached a point thirty miles beyond the Lehigh.

The Delaware Indians regarded this measurement as a pure fraud and refused to abandon the Minisink region north of the Lehigh. The

proprietors then called in the assistance of the Six
Nations of New York, who ordered the Delawares
off the Minisink lands.   Though they obeyed, the
Delawares became the relentless enemies of the
white man and in the coming years revenged themselves by massacres and murder. They also broke
the control which the Six Nations had over them,
became an independent nation, and in the French
Wars revenged themselves on the Six Nations as
well as on the white men.

The congress which convened at Albany in 1754
was an attempt on the part of the British Government to settle all Indian affairs in a general agreement and to prevent separate treaties by the different colonies; but the Pennsylvania delegates, by various devices of compass courses which the Indians
did not understand and by failing to notify and secure the consent of certain tribes, obtained a grant
of pretty much the whole of Pennsylvania west
of the Susquehanna.   The Indians considered this
procedure to be another gross fraud. It is to
be noticed that in their dealings with Penn they
had always been satisfied, and that he had always
been careful that they should be duly consulted
and if necessary be paid twice over for the land.
But his sons were more economical, and as a

result of the shrewd practices of the Albany purchase the Pennsylvania Indians almost immediately went over in a body to the French and were
soon scalping men, women, and children among
the Pennsylvania colonists.

It is a striking fact, however, that in all the
after years of war and rapine and for generations
afterwards the Indians retained the most distinct
and positive tradition of Penn's good faith and
of the honesty of all Quakers. So persistent, indeed, was this tradition among the tribes of the
West that more than a century later President
Grant proposed to put the whole charge of the
nation's Indian affairs in the hands of the Quakers.

The first efforts to avert the catastrophe threatened by the alliance of the red man with the French
were made by the provincial assemblies, which
voted presents of money or goods to the Indians
to offset similar presents from the French. The
result was, of course, the utter demoralization of
the savages. Bribed by both sides, the Indians
used all their native cunning to encourage the
bribers to bid against each other. So far as Pennsylvania was concerned, feeling themselves cheated
in the first instance and now bribed with gifts,
they developed a contempt for the people who

could stoop to such practices. As a result this contempt manifested itself in deeds hitherto unknown in the province. One tribe on a visit to Philadelphia killed cattle and robbed orchards as they passed. The delegates of another tribe, having visited Philadelphia and received £500 as a present, returned to the frontier and on their way back for another present destroyed the property of the interpreter and Indian agent, Conrad Weiser. They felt that they could do as they pleased. To make matters worse, the Assembly paid for all the damage done; and having started on this foolish business, they found that the list of tribes demanding presents rapidly increased. The Shawanoes and the Six Nations, as well as the Delawares, were now swarming to this new and convenient source of wealth.

Whether the proprietors or the Assembly should meet this increasing expense or divide it between them, became a subject of increasing controversy. It was in these discussions that Thomas Penn, in trying to keep his family's share of the expense as small as possible, first got the reputation for closeness which followed him for the rest of his life and which started a party in the province desirous of having Parliament abolish the proprietorship and put the province under a governor appointed by the Crown.

The war with the French of Canada and their Indian allies is of interest here only in so far as it affected the government of Pennsylvania. From this point of view it involved a series of contests between the proprietors and the Crown on the one side and the Assembly on the other. The proprietors and the Crown took advantage of every military necessity to force the Assembly into a surrender of popular rights. But the Assembly resisted, maintaining that they had the same right as the British Commons of having their money bills received or rejected by the Governor without amendment. Whatever they should give must be given on their own terms or not at all; and they would not yield this point to any necessities of the war.

When Governor Morris asked the Assembly for a war contribution in 1754, they promptly voted £20,000. This was the same amount that Virginia, the most active of the colonies in the war, was giving. Other colonies gave much less; New York, only £5000, and Maryland £6000. Morris, however, would not assent to the Assembly's bill unless it contained a clause suspending its effect until the King's pleasure was known. This was an attempt to establish a precedent for giving up the Assembly's charter right of passing laws which need not be submitted to the King for five years and which in the meantime were valid. The members of the Assembly very naturally refused to be forced by the necessities of the war into surrendering one of the most important privileges the province possessed. It was, they said, as much their duty to resist this invasion of their rights as to resist the French.

Governor Morris, besides demanding that the supply of £20,000 should not go into force until the King's pleasure was known, insisted that the paper money representing it should be redeemable in five years. This period the Assembly considered too short; the usual time was ten years. Five years would ruin too many people by foreclosures. Moreover, the Governor was attempting to dictate the way in which the people should raise a money supply. He and the King had a right to ask for aid in war; but it was the right of the colony to use its own methods of furnishing this assistance. The Governor also refused to let the Assembly see the instructions from the proprietors under which he was acting. This was

another attack upon their liberties and involved
nothing less than an attempt to change their charter rights by secret instructions to a deputy governor which he must obey at his peril. Several bills
had recently been introduced in the English Parliament for the purpose of making royal instructions to governors binding on all the colonial
assemblies without regard to their charters. This
innovation, the colonists felt, would wreck all
their liberties and turn colonial government into
a mere despotism.

The assemblies of all the colonies have been
a good deal abused for delay in supporting the
war and meanness in withholding money. But in
many instances the delay and lack of money were
occasioned by the grasping schemes of governors
who saw a chance to gain new privileges for the
Crown or a proprietor or to weaken popular government by crippling the powers of the legislatures.
The usual statement that the Pennsylvania Assembly was slow in assisting the war because it
was composed of Quakers is not supported by the
facts. The Pennsylvania Assembly was not behind the rest. On this particular occasion, when
their large money supply bill could not be passed
without sacrificing their constitutional rights, they

raised money for the war by appointing a committee which was authorized to borrow £5000 on the credit of the Assembly.

Other contests arose over the claim of the proprietors that their estates in the province were exempt from taxation for the war or any purpose. One bill taxing the proprietary estates along with others was met by Thomas Penn offering to subscribe £5000, as a free gift to the colony's war measures. The Assembly accepted this, and passed the bill without taxing the proprietary estates. It turned out, however, to be a shrewd business move on the part of Thomas Penn; for the £5000 was to be collected out of the quit-rents that were in arrears, and the payment of it was in consequence long delayed. The thrifty Thomas had thus saddled his bad debts on the province and gained a reputation for generosity at the same time.

Pennsylvania, though governed by Quakers assisted by noncombatant Germans, had a better protected frontier than Maryland or Virginia; no colony, indeed, was at that time better protected. The Quaker Assembly did more than take care of the frontier during the war; it preserved at the same time constitutional rights in defense of which twenty-five years afterwards the whole continent fought the Revolution. The Quaker Assembly even passed two militia bills, one of which became law, and sent rather more than the province's full share of troops to protect the frontiers of New York and New England and to carry the invasion into Canada.

General Braddock warmly praised the assistance which Pennsylvania gave him because, he said, she had done more for him than any of the other colonies. Virginia and Maryland promised everything and performed nothing, while Pennsylvania promised nothing and performed everything. Commodore Spy thanked the Assembly for the large number of sailors sent his fleet at the expense of the province. General Shirley, in charge of the New England and New York campaigns, thanked the Assembly for the numerous recruits; and it was the common opinion at the time that Pennsylvania had sent more troops to the war than any other colony. In the first four years of the war the province spent for military purposes £210,567 sterling, which was a very considerable sum at that time for a community of less than 200,000 people. Quakers, though they hate war, will accept it when there is no escape.

The old story of the Quaker who tossed a pirate overboard, saying, "Friend, thee has no business here," gives their point of view better than pages of explanation. Quaker opinion has not always been entirely uniform. In Revolutionary times in Philadelphia there was a division of the Quakers known as the Fighting Quakers, and their meeting house is still pointed out at the corner of Fifth Street and Arch. They even produced able military leaders: Colonel John Dickinson, General Greene, and General Mifflin in the Continental Army, and, in the War of 1812, General Jacob Brown, who reorganized the army and restored its failing fortunes after many officers had been tried and found wanting.

There was always among the Quakers a rationalistic party and a party of mysticism. The rationalistic party prevailed in Pennsylvania all through the colonial period. In the midst of the worst horrors of the French and Indian wars, however, the conscientious objectors roused themselves and began preaching and exhorting what has been called the mystical side of the faith. Many extreme Quaker members of the Assembly resigned their seats in consequence. After the Revolution the spiritual party began gaining ground, partly perhaps because then the responsibilities of government and care of the great political and religious experiment in Pennsylvania were removed. The spiritual party increased so rapidly in power that in 1827 a split occurred which involved not a little bitterness, ill feeling, and litigation over property. This division into two opposing camps, known as the Hicksites and the Orthodox, continues and is likely to remain.

Quaker government in Pennsylvania was put to still severer tests by the difficulties and disasters that followed Braddock's defeat. That unfortunate general had something over two thousand men and was hampered with a train of artillery and a splendid equipment of arms, tools, and supplies, as if he were to march over the smooth highways of Europe. When he came to drag all these munitions through the depths of the Pennsylvania forests and up and down the mountains, he found that he made only about three miles a day and that his horses had nothing to eat but the leaves of the trees. Washington, who was of the party, finally persuaded him to abandon his artillery and press forward with about fifteen hundred picked men. These troops, when a few miles from Fort Duquesne (now Pittsburgh), met about six hundred Indians and three hundred French coming from the fort. The English maintained a close formation where they were, but the French and Indians immediately spread out on their flanks, lying behind trees and logs which provided rests for their rifles and security for their bodies. This strategy decided the day. The English were shot down like cattle in a pen, and out of about fifteen hundred only four hundred and fifty escaped. The French and Indian loss was not much over fifty.

This defeat of Braddock's force has become one of the most famous reverses in history; and it was made worse by the conduct of Dunbar who had been left in command of the artillery, baggage, and men in the rear. He could have remained where he was as some sort of protection to the frontier. But he took fright, burned his wagons, emptied his barrels of powder into the streams, destroyed his provisions, and fled back to Fort Cumberland in Maryland. Here the governors of Pennsylvania and Virginia as well as the Pennsylvania Assembly urged him to stay. But determined to make the British rout complete, he soon retreated to the peace and quiet of Philadelphia, and nothing would induce him to enter again the terrible forests of Pennsylvania.

The natural result of the blunder soon followed. The French, finding the whole frontier of Pennsylvania, Maryland, and Virginia abandoned, organized the Indians under French officers and swept the whole region with a devastation of massacre, scalping, and burning that has never been equaled. Hurons, Potawatomies, Ojibways, Ottawas, Mingoes, renegades from the Six Nations, together with the old treaty friends of Penn, the Delawares and Shawanoes, began swarming eastward and soon had killed more people than had been lost at Braddock's defeat. The onslaught reached its height in September and October. By that time all the outlying frontier settlers and their families had been killed or sent flying eastward to seek refuge in the settlements. The Indians even followed them to the settlements, reached the Susquehanna, and crossed it. They massacred the people of the village of Gnadenhütten, near Bethlehem on the Lehigh, and established near by a headquarters for prisoners and plunder. Families were scalped within fifty miles of Philadelphia, and in one instance the bodies of a murdered family were brought into the town and exhibited in the streets to show the inhabitants how near the danger was approaching.

Nothing could be done to stem the savage tide. Virginia was suffering in the same way: the settlers on her border were slaughtered or were driven back in herds upon the more settled districts, and Washington, with a nominal strength of fifteen hundred who would not obey orders, was forced to stand a helpless spectator of the general flight and misery.   There was no adequate force or army anywhere within reach. The British had been put to flight and had gone to the defense of New England and New York. Neither Pennsylvania nor Virginia had a militia that could withstand the French and their red allies. They could only wait till the panic had subsided and then see what could be done.

One thing was accomplished, however, when the Pennsylvania Assembly passed a Quaker militia law which is one of the most curious legal documents of its kind in history. It was most aptly worded, drafted by the master hand of Franklin. It recited the fact that the province had always been ruled by Quakers who were opposed to war, but that now it had become necessary to allow men to become soldiers and to give them every facility for the profession of arms, because the Assembly though containing a Quaker majority nevertheless represented all the people of the province. To prevent those who believed in war from taking part in it would be as much a violation of liberty of conscience as to force enlistments among those who had conscientious scruples against it. Nor would the Quaker majority have any right to compel others to bear arms and at the same time exempt themselves. Therefore a voluntary militia system was established under which a fighting Quaker, a Presbyterian, an Episcopalian, or anybody, could enlist and have all the military glory he could win.

It was altogether a volunteer system. Two years afterwards, as the necessities of war increased, the Quaker Assembly passed a rather stringent compulsory militia bill; but the governor vetoed it, and the first law with its volunteer system remained in force. Franklin busied himself to encourage enlistments under it and was very successful. Though a philosopher and a man of science, almost as much opposed to war as the Quakers and not even owning a shotgun, he was elected commander and led a force of about five hundred men to protect the Lehigh Valley. His common sense seems to have supplied his lack of military training. He did no worse than some professional soldiers who might be named. The valley was supposed to be in great danger since its village of Gnadenhütten had been burned and its people massacred. The Moravians, like the Quakers, had suddenly found that they were not as much opposed to war as they had supposed. They had obtained arms and ammunition from New York and had built stockades, and Franklin was glad to find them so well prepared when he arrived. He built small forts in different parts of the valley, acted entirely on the defensive, and no doubt checked the raids of the Indians at that point. They seem to have been watching him from the hilltops all the time, and any rashness on his part would probably have brought disaster upon him. After his force had been withdrawn, the Indians again attacked and burned Gnadenhütten.

The chain of forts, at first seventeen, afterwards increased to fifty, built by the Assembly on the Pennsylvania frontier was a good plan so far as it went, but it was merely defensive and by no means completely defensive, since Indian raiding parties could pass between the forts. They served chiefly as refuges for neighboring settlers. The colonial troops or militia, after manning the fifty forts and sending their quota to the operations against Canada by way of New England and New York, were not numerous enough to attack the Indians. They could only act on the defensive as Franklin's command had done. As for the rangers, as the small bands of frontiersmen acting without any authority of either governor or legislature were called, they were very efficient as individuals but they accomplished very little because they acted at widely isolated spots. What was needed was a well organized force which could pursue the Indians on their own ground so far westward that the settlers on the frontier would be safe. The only troops which could do this were the British regulars with the assistance of the colonial militia.

Two energetic efforts to end the war without aid from abroad were made, however, one by the pacific Quakers and the other by the combatant portion of the people. Both of these were successful so far as they went, but had little effect on the general situation. In the summer of 1756, the Quakers made a very earnest effort to persuade the two principal Pennsylvania tribes, the Delawares and Shawanoes, to withdraw from the French alliance and return to their old friends. These two tribes possessed a knowledge of the country which enabled them greatly to assist the

French designs on Pennsylvania. Chiefs of these tribes were brought under safe conducts to Philadelphia, where they were entertained as equals in the Quaker homes. Such progress, indeed, was made that by the end of July a treaty of peace was concluded at Easton eliminating those two tribes from the war. This has sometimes been sneered at as mere Quaker pacifism; but it was certainly successful in lessening the numbers and effectiveness of the enemy.

The other undertaking was a military one, the famous attack upon Kittanning conducted by Colonel John Armstrong, an Ulsterman from Carlisle, Pennsylvania, and the first really aggressive officer the province had produced. The Indians had two headquarters for their raids into the province, one at Logstown on the Ohio a few miles below Fort Duquesne, and the other at Kittanning or, as the French called it, Attiqué, about forty miles northeast. At these two points they assembled their forces, received ammunition and supplies from the French, and organized their expeditions. As Kittanning was the nearer, Armstrong in a masterly maneuver took three hundred men through the mountains without being discovered and, by falling upon the village early in the morning, he effected a complete surprise. The town was set on fire, the Indians were put to flight, and large quantities of their ammunition were destroyed. But Armstrong could not follow up his success. Threatened by overwhelming numbers, he hastened to withdraw. The effect which the fighting and the Quaker treaty had on the frontier was good. Incursions of the savages were, at least for the present, checked. But the root of the evil had not yet been reached, and the Indians remained massed along the Ohio, ready to break in upon the people again at the first opportunity.

The following year, 1757, was the most depressing period of the war. The proprietors of Pennsylvania took the opportunity to exempt their own estate from taxation and throw the burden of furnishing money for the war upon the colonists. Under pressure of the increasing success of the French and Indians and because the dreadful massacres were coming nearer and nearer to Philadelphia, the Quaker Assembly yielded, voted the largest sum they had ever voted to the war, and exempted the proprietary estates. The colony was soon boiling with excitement. The Churchmen, as friends of the proprietors, were delighted to have the estates exempted, thought it a good opportunity to have the Quaker Assembly abolished, and sent petitions and letters and proofs of alleged Quaker incompetence to the British Government. The Quakers and a large majority of the colonists, on the other hand, instead of consenting to their own destruction, struck at the root of the Churchmen's power by proposing to abolish the proprietors. And in a letter to Isaac Norris, Benjamin Franklin, who had been sent to England to present the grievances of the colonists, even suggested that "tumults and insurrections that might prove the proprietary government unable to preserve order, or show the people to be ungovernable, would do the business immediately."

Turmoil and party strife rose to the most exciting heights, and the details of it might, under certain circumstances, be interesting to describe. But the next year, 1758, the British Government, by sending a powerful force of regulars to Pennsylvania, at last adopted the only method for ending the war. Confidence was at once restored. The Pennsylvania Assembly now voted the sufficient and, indeed, immense sum of one hundred thousand pounds, and offered a bounty of five pounds to every recruit. It was no longer a war of defense but now a war of aggression and conquest. Fort

Duquesne on the Ohio was taken; and the next autumn Fort Pitt was built on its ruins. Then Canada fell, and the French empire in America came to an end. Canada and the Great West passed into the possession of the Anglo-Saxon race.

CHAPTER VII

THE DECLINE OF QUAKER GOVERNMENT

WHEN the treaty of peace was signed in 1763, extinguishing France's title to Canada and turning over Canada and the Mississippi Valley to the English, the colonists were prepared to enjoy all the blessings of peace. But the treaty of peace had been made with France, not with the red man. A remarkable genius, Pontiac, appeared among the Indians, one of the few characters, like Tecumseh and Osceola, who are often cited as proof of latent powers almost equal to the strongest qualities of the white race. Within a few months he had united all the tribes of the West in a discipline and control which, if it had been brought to the assistance of the French six years earlier, might have conquered the colonies to the Atlantic seaboard before the British regulars could have come to their assistance. The tribes swept eastward into Pennsylvania, burning, murdering, and leveling every habitation to the ground with a thoroughness beyond anything attempted under the French alliance. The settlers and farmers fled eastward to the towns to live in cellars, camps, and sheds as best they could.[1] Fortunately the colonies retained a large part of the military organization, both men and officers, of the French War, and were soon able to handle the situation. Detroit and Niagara were relieved by water; and an expedition commanded by Colonel Bouquet, who had distinguished himself under General Forbes, saved Fort Pitt.

At this time the Scotch-Irish frontiersmen suddenly became prominent. They had been organizing for their own protection and were meeting with not a little success. They refused to join the expedition of regular troops marching westward against Pontiac's warriors, because they wanted to protect their own homes and because they believed the regulars to be marching to sure destruction. Many of the regular troops were invalided from the West Indies, and the Scotch-Irish never expected to see any of them again. They believed that the salvation of Pennsylvania,

---

[1] For an account of Pontiac's conspiracy, see *The Old Northwest*, by Frederic A. Ogg (in *The Chronicles of America*).

or at least of their part of the province, depended
entirely upon themselves. Their increasing numbers and rugged independence were forming them
also into an organized political party with decided
tendencies, as it afterwards appeared, towards
forming a separate state.

The extreme narrowness of the Scotch-Irish, however, misled them. The only real safety for the
province lay in regularly constituted and strong
expeditions, like that of Bouquet, which would
drive the main body of the savages far westward.
But the Scotch-Irish could not see this; and with
that intensity of passion which marked all their
actions they turned their energy and vengeance
upon the Quakers and semicivilized Indians in
the eastern end of the colony. Their preachers,
who were their principal leaders and organizers,
encouraged them in denouncing Quaker doctrine
as a wicked heresy from which only evil could
result. The Quakers had offended God from the
beginning by making treaties of kindness with the
heathen savages instead of exterminating them
as the Scripture commanded: *"And when the
Lord thy God shall deliver them before thee, thou
shalt smite them and utterly destroy them; thou shalt
make no covenant with them, nor show mercy unto*

them." The Scripture had not been obeyed; the
heathen had not been destroyed; on the contrary,
a systematic policy of covenants, treaties, and
kindness had been persisted in for two generations, and as a consequence, the Ulstermen said,
the frontiers were now deluged in blood. They
were particularly resentful against the small settlement of Indians near Bethlehem, who had
been converted to Christianity by the Moravians,
and another little village of half civilized basket-
making Indians at Conestoga near Lancaster.
The Scotch-Irish had worked themselves up into
a strange belief that these small remnants were
sending information, arms, and ammunition to the
western tribes; and they seemed to think that it
was more important to exterminate these little
communities than to go with such expeditions as
Bouquet's to the West. They asked the Governor
to remove these civilized Indians and assured him
that their removal would secure the safety of the
frontier. When the Governor, not being able to
find anything against the Indians, declined to remove them, the Scotch-Irish determined to attend
to the matter in their own fashion.

Bouquet's victory at Bushy Run, much to the
surprise of the Scotch-Irish, stopped Indian raids

of any seriousness until the following spring. But in the autumn there were a few depredations, which led the frontiersmen to believe that the whole invasion would begin again. A party of them, therefore, started to attack the Moravian Indians near Bethlehem; but before they could accomplish their object, the Governor brought most of the Indians down to Philadelphia for protection. Even there they were narrowly saved from the mob, for the hostility against them was spreading throughout the province.

Soon afterwards another party of Scotch-Irish, ever since known as the "Paxton Boys," went at break of day to the village of the Conestoga Indians and found only six of them at home — three men, two women, and a boy. These they instantly shot down, mutilated their bodies, and burned their cabins. As the murderers returned, they related to a man on the road what they had done, and when he protested against the cruelty of the deed, they asked, "Don't you believe in God and the Bible?" The remaining fourteen inhabitants of the village, who were away selling brooms, were collected by the sheriff and put in the jail at Lancaster for protection. The Paxtons heard of it and in a few days stormed the jail, broke down the doors, and either shot the poor Indians or cut them to pieces with hatchets.

This was probably the first instance of lynch law in America. It raised a storm of indignation and controversy; and a pamphlet war persisted for several years. The whole province was immediately divided into two parties. On one side were the Quakers, most of the Germans, and conservatives of every sort, and on the other, inclined to sympathize with the Scotch-Irish, were the eastern Presbyterians, some of the Churchmen, and various miscellaneous people whose vindictiveness towards all Indians had been aroused by the war. The Quakers and conservatives, who seem to have been the more numerous, assailed the Scotch-Irish in no measured language as a gang of ruffians without respect for law or order who, though always crying for protection, had refused to march with Bouquet to save Fort Pitt or to furnish him the slightest assistance. Instead of going westward where the danger was and something might be accomplished, they had turned eastward among the settlements and murdered a few poor defenseless people, mostly women and children.

Franklin, who had now returned from England, wrote one of his best pamphlets against the

8

Paxtons, the valorous, heroic Paxtons, as he called
them, prating of God and the Bible, fifty-seven of
whom, armed with rifles, knives, and hatchets,
had actually succeeded in killing three old men,
two women, and a boy. This pamphlet became
known as the *Narrative* from the first word of its
title, and it had an immense circulation. Like
everything Franklin wrote, it is interesting reading
to this day.

One of the first effects of this controversy was
to drive the excitable Scotch-Irish into a flame
of insurrection not unlike the Whisky Rebellion,
which started among them some years after the
Revolution. They held tumultuous meetings denouncing the Quakers and the whole proprietary
government in Philadelphia, and they organized
an expedition which included some delegates to
suggest reforms. For the most part, however, it
was a well equipped little army variously estimated at from five hundred to fifteen hundred on
foot and on horseback, which marched towards
Philadelphia with no uncertain purpose. They
openly declared that they intended to capture the
town, seize the Moravian Indians protected there,
and put them to death. They fully expected to
be supported by most of the people and to have

everything their own way. As they passed along
the roads, they amused themselves in their rough
fashion by shooting chickens and pigs, frighten-
ing people by thrusting their rifles into windows,
and occasionally throwing some one down and
pretending to scalp him.

In the city there was great excitement and
alarm. Even the classes who sympathized with
the Scotch-Irish did not altogether relish having
their property burned or destroyed. Great preparations were made to meet the expedition. British regulars were summoned. Eight companies
of militia and a battery of artillery were hastily
formed. Franklin became a military man once
more and superintended the preparations. On
all sides the Quakers were enlisting; they had
become accustomed to war; and this legitimate
chance to shoot a Scotch-Irish Presbyterian was
too much for the strongest scruples of their religion.
It was a long time, however, before they heard
the end of this zeal; and in the pamphlet war
which followed they were accused of clamorously
rushing to arms and demanding to be led against
the enemy.

It is amusing now to read about it in the old
records. But it was serious enough at the time.

When the Scotch-Irish army reached the Schuyl-kill River and found the fords leading to the city guarded, they were not quite so enthusiastic about killing Quakers and Indians. They went up the river some fifteen miles, crossed by an unopposed ford, and halted in Germantown ten miles north of Philadelphia. That was as far as they thought it safe to venture. Several days passed, during which the city people continued their preparations and expected every night to be attacked. There were, indeed, several false alarms. Whenever the alarm was sounded at night, every one placed candles in his windows to light up the streets. One night when it rained the soldiers were allowed to shelter themselves in a Quaker meeting house, which for some hours bristled with bayonets and swords, an incident of which the Presbyterian pamphleteers afterwards made much use for satire. On another day all the cannon were fired to let the enemy know what was in store for him.

Finally commissioners with the clever, genial Franklin at their head, went out to Germantown to negotiate, and soon had the whole mighty dif-ference composed. The Scotch-Irish stated their grievances. The Moravian Indians ought not to be protected by the government, and all such

Indians should be removed from the colony; the men who killed the Conestoga Indians should be tried where the supposed offense was committed and not in Philadelphia; the five frontier counties had only ten representatives in the Assembly while the three others had twenty-six — this should be remedied; men wounded in border war should be cared for at public expense; no trade should be carried on with hostile Indians until they restored prisoners; and there should be a bounty on scalps.

While these negotiations were proceeding, some of the Scotch-Irish amused themselves by practicing with their rifles at the weather vane, a figure of a cock, on the steeple of the old Lutheran church in Germantown — an unimportant incident, it is true, but one revealing the conditions and character of the time as much as graver matters do. The old weather vane with the bullet marks upon it is still preserved. About thirty of these same riflemen were invited to Philadelphia and were allowed to wander about and see the sights of the town. The rest returned to the frontier. As for their list of grievances, not one of them was granted except, strange and sad to relate, the one which asked for a scalp bounty. The Governor, after the manner of other colonies, it must be admitted, issued the long desired scalp proclamation, which after offering rewards for prisoners and scalps, closed by saying, "and for the scalp of a female Indian fifty pieces of eight." William Penn's Indian policy had been admired for its justice and humanity by all the philosophers and statesmen of the world, and now his grandson, Governor of the province, in the last days of the family's control, was offering bounties for women's scalps.

Franklin while in England had succeeded in having the proprietary lands taxed equally with the lands of the colonists. But the proprietors attempted to construe this provision so that their best lands were taxed at the rate paid by the people on their worst. This obvious quibble of course raised such a storm of opposition that the Quakers, joined by classes which had never before supported them, and now forming a large majority, determined to appeal to the Government in England to abolish the proprietorship and put the colony under the rule of the King. In the proposal to make Pennsylvania a Crown colony there was no intention of confiscating the possessions of the proprietors. It was merely the proprietary political power, their right to appoint the Governor, that was to be abolished. This right was to be absorbed by the Crown with payment for its value to the proprietors; but in all other respects the charter and the rights and liberties of the people were to remain unimpaired. Just there lay the danger. An act of Parliament would be required to make the change and, having once started on such a change, Parliament, or the party in power therein, might decide to make other changes, and in the end there might remain very little of the original rights and liberties of the colonists under their charter. It was by no means a wise move. But intense feeling on the subject was aroused. Passionate feeling seemed to have been running very high among the steady Quakers. In this new outburst the Quakers had the Scotch-Irish on their side, and a part of the Churchmen. The Germans were divided. But the majority enthusiastic for the change was very large.

There was a new alinement of parties. The eastern Presbyterians, usually more or less in sympathy with the Scotch-Irish, broke away from them on this occasion. These Presbyterians opposed the change to a royal governor because they believed that it would be followed by the establishment by law of the Church of England, with bishops and all the other ancient evils. Although some of the Churchmen joined the Quaker side, most of them and the most influential of them were opposed to the change and did good work in opposing it. They were well content with their position under the proprietors and saw nothing to be gained under a royal governor. There were also not a few people who, in the increase of the wealth of the province, had acquired aristocratic tastes and were attached to the pleasant social conditions that had grown up round the proprietary governors and their followers; and there were also those whose salaries, incomes, or opportunities for wealth were more or less dependent on the proprietors retaining the executive offices and the appointments and patronage.

One of the most striking instances of a change of sides was the case of a Philadelphia Quaker, John Dickinson, a lawyer of large practice, a man of wealth and position, and of not a little colonial magnificence when he drove in his coach and four. It was he who later wrote the famous *Farmer's Letters* during the Revolution. He was a member of the Assembly and had been in politics for some years. But on this question of a change to royal government, he left the Quaker majority and opposed the change with all his influence and ability.

He and his father-in-law, Isaac Norris, Speaker of the Assembly, became the leaders against the change, and Franklin and Joseph Galloway, the latter afterwards a prominent loyalist in the Revolution, were the leading advocates of the change.

The whole subject was thoroughly thrashed out in debates in the Assembly and in pamphlets of very great ability and of much interest to students of colonial history and the growth of American ideas of liberty. It must be remembered that this was the year 1764, on the eve of the Revolution. British statesmen were planning a system of more rigorous control of the colonies; and the advisability of a stamp tax was under consideration. Information of all these possible changes had reached the colonies. Dickinson foresaw the end and warned the people. Franklin and the Quaker party thought there was no danger and that the mother country could be implicitly trusted.

Dickinson warned the people that the British Ministry were starting special regulations for new colonies and "designing the strictest reformations in the old." It would be a great relief, he admitted, to be rid of the pettiness of the proprietors, and it might be accomplished some time in the future; but not now. The proprietary system might be bad, but a royal government might be worse and might wreck all the liberties of the province, religious freedom, the Assembly's control of its own adjournments, and its power of raising and disposing of the public money. The ministry of the day in England were well known not to be favorably inclined towards Pennsylvania because of the frequently reported willfulness of the Assembly, on which the recent disturbances had also been blamed. If the King, Ministry, and Parliament started upon a change, they might decide to reconstitute the Assembly entirely, abolish its ancient privileges, and disfranchise both Quakers and Presbyterians.

The arguments of Franklin and Galloway consisted principally of assertions of the good intentions of the mother country and the absurdity of any fear on the part of the colonists for their privileges. But the King in whom they had so much confidence was George III, and the Parliament which they thought would do no harm was the same one which a few months afterwards passed the Stamp Act which brought on the Revolution. Franklin and Galloway also asserted that the colonies like Massachusetts, the Jerseys, and the Carolinas, which had been changed to royal governments, had profited by the change. But that was hardly the prevailing opinion in those colonies themselves. Royal governors could be as petty and annoying as the Penns and far more tyrannical. Pennsylvania had always defeated any attempts at despotism on the part of the Penn family and had built up a splendid body of liberal laws and legislative privileges. But governors with the authority and power of the British Crown behind them could not be so easily resisted as the deputy governors of the Penns.

The Assembly, however, voted — twenty-seven to three — with Franklin and Galloway. In the general election of the autumn, the question was debated anew among the people and, though Franklin and Galloway were defeated for seats in the Assembly, yet the popular verdict was strongly in favor of a change, and the majority in the Assembly was for practical purposes unaltered. They voted to appeal to England for the change, and appointed Franklin to be their agent before the Crown and Ministry. He sailed again for England and soon was involved in the opening scenes of the Revolution. He was made agent for all the colonies and he spent many delightful years there pursuing his studies in science, dining with distinguished men, staying at country seats, and learning all the arts of diplomacy for which he afterwards became so distinguished.

As for the Assembly's petition for a change to royal government, Franklin presented it but never pressed it. He, too, was finally convinced that the time was inopportune. In fact, the Assembly itself before long began to have doubts and fears and sent him word to let the subject drop; and amid much greater events it was soon entirely forgotten.

CHAPTER VIII

THE BEGINNINGS OF NEW JERSEY

NEW JERSEY, Scheyichbi, as the Indians called it, or Nova Cæsarea, as it was called in the Latin of its proprietary grant, had a history rather different from that of other English colonies in America. Geographically, it had not a few attractions. It was a good sized dominion surrounded on all sides but one by water, almost an island domain, secluded and independent. In fact, it was the only one of the colonies which stood naturally separate and apart. The others were bounded almost entirely by artificial or imaginary lines.

It offered an opportunity, one might have supposed, for some dissatisfied religious sect of the seventeenth century to secure a sanctuary and keep off all intruders. But at first no one of the various denominations seems to have fancied it or chanced upon it. The Puritans disembarked upon the bleak shores of New England well suited to the sternness of their religion. How different American history might have been if they had established themselves in the Jerseys! Could they, under those milder skies, have developed witchcraft, set up blue laws, and indulged in the killing of Quakers? After a time they learned about the Jerseys and cast thrifty eyes upon them. Their seafaring habits and the pursuit of whales led them along the coast and into Delaware Bay. The Puritans of New Haven made persistent efforts to settle the southern part of Jersey, on the Delaware near Salem. They thought, as their quaint old records show, that if they could once start a branch colony in Jersey it might become more populous and powerful than the New Haven settlement and in that case they intended to move their seat of government to the new colony. But their shrewd estimate of its value came too late. The Dutch and the Swedes occupied the Delaware at that time and drove them out. Puritans, however, entered northern Jersey and, while they were not numerous enough to make it a thoroughly Puritan community, they largely tinged its thought and its laws, and their influence still survives.

The difficulty with Jersey was that its seacoast was a monotonous line of breakers with dangerous shoal inlets, few harbors, and vast mosquito infested salt marshes and sandy thickets. In the interior it was for the most part a level, heavily forested, sandy, swampy country in its southern portions, and rough and mountainous in the northern portions. Even the entrance by Delaware Bay was so difficult by reason of its shoals that it was the last part of the coast to be explored. The Delaware region and Jersey were in fact a sort of middle ground far less easy of access by the sea than the regions to the north in New England and to the south in Virginia.

There were only two places easy of settlement in the Jerseys. One was the open region of meadows and marshes by Newark Bay near the mouth of the Hudson and along the Hackensack River, whence the people slowly extended themselves to the seashore at Sandy Hook and thence southward along the ocean beach. This was East Jersey. The other easily occupied region, which became West Jersey, stretched along the shore of the lower Delaware from the modern Trenton to Salem, whence the settlers gradually worked their way into the interior. Between these two divisions lay a rough wilderness which in its southern portion was full of swamps, thickets, and pine barrens. So rugged was the country that the native Indians lived for the most part only in the two open regions already described.

The natural geographical, geological, and even social division of New Jersey is made by drawing a line from Trenton to the mouth of the Hudson River. North of that line the successive terraces of the piedmont and mountainous region form part of the original North American continent. South of that line the more or less sandy level region was once a shoal beneath the ocean; afterwards a series of islands; then one island with a wide sound behind it passing along the division line to the mouth of the Hudson. Southern Jersey was in short an island with a sound behind it very much like the present Long Island. The shoal and island had been formed in the far distant geologic past by the erosion and washings from the lofty Pennsylvania mountains now worn down to mere stumps.

The Delaware River flowed into this sound at Trenton. Gradually the Hudson end of the sound filled up as far as Trenton, but the tide from the ocean still runs up the remains of the Old Sound as far as Trenton. The Delaware should still be properly considered as ending at Trenton, for the rest of its course to the ocean is still part of Old Pensauken Sound, as it is called by geologists.

The Jerseys originated as a colony in 1664. In 1675 West Jersey passed into the control of the Quakers. In 1680 East Jersey came partially under Quaker influence. In August, 1664, Charles II seized New York, New Jersey, and all the Dutch possessions in America, having previously in March granted them to his brother the Duke of York. The Duke almost immediately gave to Lord Berkeley and Sir George Carteret, members of the Privy Council and defenders of the Stuart family in the Cromwellian wars, the land between the Delaware River and the ocean, and bounded on the north by a line drawn from latitude 41° on the Hudson to latitude 41° 40′ on the Delaware. This region was to be called, the grant said, Nova Cæsarea, or New Jersey. The name was a compliment to Carteret, who in the Cromwellian wars had defended the little isle of Jersey against the forces of the Long Parliament. As the American Jersey was then almost an island and geologically had been one, the name was not inappropriate.

Berkeley and Carteret divided the province between them. In 1676 an exact division was attempted, creating the rather unnatural sections

known as East Jersey and West Jersey. The
first idea seems to have been to divide by a line
running from Barnegat on the seashore to the
mouth of Pensauken Creek on the Delaware just
above Camden. This, however, would have made
a North Jersey and a South Jersey, with the latter
much smaller than the former. Several lines seem
to have been surveyed at different times in the
attempt to make an exactly equal division, which
was no easy engineering task. As private land
titles and boundaries were in some places dependent on the location of the division line, there
resulted much controversy and litigation which
lasted down into our own time. Without going
into details, it is sufficient to say that the accept-
able division line began on the seashore at Little
Egg Harbor at the lower end of Barnegat Bay and
crossed diagonally or northwesterly to the northern
part of the Delaware River just above the Water
Gap. It is known as the Old Province line, and
it can be traced on any map of the State by
prolonging, in both directions, the northeastern
boundary of Burlington County.

West Jersey, which became decidedly Quaker,
did not remain long in the possession of Lord

Berkeley. He was growing old; and, disappointed in his hopes of seeing it settled, he sold it, in 1673, for one thousand pounds to John Fenwick and Edward Byllinge, both of them old Cromwellian soldiers turned Quakers. That this purchase was made for the purpose of affording a refuge in America for Quakers then much imprisoned and persecuted in England does not very distinctly appear. At least there was no parade of it. But such a purpose in addition to profit for the proprietors may well have been in the minds of the purchasers.

George Fox, the Quaker leader, had just returned from a missionary journey in America, in the course of which he had traveled through New Jersey in going from New York to Maryland. Some years previously in England, about 1659, he had made inquiries as to a suitable place for Quaker settlement and was told of the region north of Maryland which became Pennsylvania. But how could a persecuted sect obtain such a region from the British Crown and the Government that was persecuting them? It would require powerful influence at Court; nothing could then be done about it; and Pennsylvania had to wait until William Penn became a man with influence

enough in 1681 to win it from the Crown. But
here was West Jersey, no longer owned directly
by the Crown and bought in cheap by two Quakers. It was an unexpected opportunity. Quakers soon went to it, and it was the first Quaker
colonial experiment.

Byllinge and Fenwick, though turned Quakers,
seem to have retained some of the contentious
Cromwellian spirit of their youth. They soon
quarreled over their respective interests in the
ownership of West Jersey; and to prevent a law-
suit, so objectionable to Quakers, the decision was
left to William Penn, then a rising young Quaker
about thirty years old, dreaming of ideal colonies
in America. Penn awarded Fenwick a one-tenth
interest and four hundred pounds. Byllinge soon
became insolvent and turned over his nine-tenths
interest to his creditors, appointing Penn and two
other Quakers, Gawen Lawrie, a merchant of
London, and Nicholas Lucas, a maltster of Hert-
ford, to hold it in trust for them. Gawen Lawrie
afterwards became deputy governor of East Jersey.
Lucas was one of those thoroughgoing Quakers just
released from eight years in prison for his religion.[1]

[1] Myers, *Narratives of Early Pennsylvania, West Jersey, and Delaware*, p. 180.

Fenwick also in the end fell into debt and, after selling over one hundred thousand acres to about fifty purchasers, leased what remained of his interest for a thousand years to John Edridge, a tanner, and Edmund Warner, a poulterer, as security for money borrowed from them. They conveyed this lease and their claims to Penn, Lawrie, and Lucas, who thus became the owners, as trustees, of pretty much all West Jersey.

This was William Penn's first practical experience in American affairs. He and his fellow trustees, with the consent of Fenwick, divided the West Jersey ownership into one hundred shares. The ninety belonging to Byllinge were offered for sale to settlers or to creditors of Byllinge who would take them in exchange for debts. The settlement of West Jersey thus became the distribution of an insolvent Quaker's estate among his creditor fellow religionists.

Although no longer in possession of a title to land, Fenwick, in 1675, went out with some Quaker settlers to Delaware Bay. There they founded the modern town of Salem, which means peace, giving it that name because of the fair and peaceful aspect of the wilderness on the day they arrived. They bought the land from the Indians in the usual manner, as the Swedes and Dutch had so often done. But they had no charter or provision for organized government. When Fenwick attempted to exercise political authority at Salem, he was seized and imprisoned by Andros, Governor of New York for the Duke of York, on the ground that, although the Duke had given Jersey to certain individual proprietors, the political control of it remained in the Duke's deputy governor. Andros, who had levied a tax of five per cent on all goods passing up the Delaware, now established commissioners at Salem to collect the duties.

This action brought up the whole question of the authority of Andros. The trustee proprietors of West Jersey appealed to the Duke of York, who was suspiciously indifferent to the matter, but finally referred it for decision to a prominent lawyer, Sir William Jones, before whom the Quaker proprietors of West Jersey made a most excellent argument. They showed the illegality, injustice, and wrong of depriving the Jerseys of vested political rights and forcing them from the freeman's right of making their own laws to a state of mere dependence on the arbitrary will of one man. Then with much boldness they declared that "To exact such an unterminated tax from English planters, and to continue it after so many repeated complaints, will be the greatest evidence of a design to introduce, if the Crown should ever devolve upon the Duke, an unlimited government in old England." Prophetic words which the Duke, in a few years, tried his best to fulfill. But Sir William Jones deciding against him, he acquiesced, confirmed the political rights of West Jersey by a separate grant, and withdrew any authority Andros claimed over East Jersey. The trouble, however, did not end here. Both the Jerseys were long afflicted by domineering attempts from New York.

Penn and his fellow trustees now prepared a constitution, or *Concessions and Agreements*, as they called it, for West Jersey, the first Quaker political constitution embodying their advanced ideas, establishing religious liberty, universal suffrage, and voting by ballot, and abolishing imprisonment for debt. It foreshadowed some of the ideas subsequently included in the Pennsylvania constitution. All these experiences were an excellent school for William Penn. He learned the importance in starting a colony of having a carefully and maturely considered system of government. In his preparations some years afterwards for establishing Pennsylvania he avoided much of the bungling of the West Jersey enterprise.

A better organized attempt was now made to establish a foothold in West Jersey farther up the river than Fenwick's colony at Salem. In 1677 the ship *Kent* took out some 230 rather well-to-do Quakers, about as fine a company of broadbrims, it is said, as ever entered the Delaware. Some were from Yorkshire and London, largely creditors of Byllinge, who were taking land to satisfy their debts. They all went up the river to Raccoon Creek on the Jersey side, about fifteen miles below the present site of Philadelphia, and lived at first among the Swedes, who had been in that part of Jersey for some years and who took care of the new arrivals in their barns and sheds. These Quaker immigrants, however, soon began to take care of themselves, and the weather during the winter proving mild, they explored farther up the river in a small boat. They bought from the Indians the land along the river shore from Oldman's Creek all the way up to Trenton and made their first settlements on the river about eighteen miles above the site of Philadelphia, at a place they at first called New Beverly, then Bridlington, and finally Burlington.

They may have chosen this spot partly because there had been an old Dutch settlement of a few families there. It had long been a crossing of the Delaware for the few persons who passed by land from New York or New England to Maryland and Virginia. One of the Dutchmen, Peter Yegon, kept a ferry and a house for entertaining travelers. George Fox, who crossed there in 1671, describes the place as having been plundered by the Indians and deserted. He and his party swam their horses across the river and got some of the Indians to help them with canoes.

Other Quaker immigrants followed, going to Salem as well as to Burlington, and a stretch of some fifty miles of the river shore became strongly Quaker. There are not many American towns now to be found with more of the old-time picturesqueness and more relics of the past than Salem and Burlington.

Settlements were also started on the river opposite the site afterwards occupied by Philadelphia, at Newton on the creek still called by that name; and another a little above on Cooper's Creek, known as Cooper's Ferry until 1794. Since then it has become the flourishing town of Camden, full of shipbuilding and manufacturing, but for long after the Revolution it was merely a small village on the Jersey shore opposite Philadelphia, sometimes used as a hunting ground and a place of resort for duelers and dancing parties from Philadelphia.

The Newton settlers were Quakers of the English middle class, weavers, tanners, carpenters, bricklayers, chandlers, blacksmiths, coopers, bakers, haberdashers, hatters, and linen drapers, most of them possessed of property in England and bringing good supplies with them. Like all the rest of the New Jersey settlers they were in no sense adventurers, gold seekers, cavaliers, or desperadoes. They were well-to-do middle class English tradespeople who would never have thought of leaving England if they had not lost faith in the stability of civil and religious liberty and the security of their property under the Stuart Kings. With them came servants, as they were called; that is, persons of no property, who agreed to work for a certain time in payment of their passage, to escape from England. All, indeed, were escaping from England before their estates melted away in fines and confiscations or their health or lives ended in the damp, foul air of the crowded prisons. Many of those who came had been in jail and had decided that they would not risk imprisonment a second time. Indeed, the proportion of West Jersey immigrants who had actually been in prison for holding or attending Quaker meetings or refusing to pay tithes for the support of the established church was large. For example, William Bates, a carpenter, while in jail for his religion, made arrangements with his friends to escape to West Jersey as soon as he should be released, and his descendants are now scattered over the United States. Robert Turner, a man of means, who settled finally in Philadelphia but also owned much land near Newton in West Jersey, had been imprisoned in England in 1660, again in 1662, again in 1665, and some of his property had been taken, again imprisoned in 1669 and more property taken; and many others had the same experience. Details such as these make us realize the situation from which the Quakers sought to escape. So widespread was the Quaker movement in England and so severe the punishment imposed in order to suppress it that fifteen thousand families are said to have been ruined by the fines, confiscations, and imprisonments.

Not a few Jersey Quakers were from Ireland, whither they had fled because there the laws

against them were less rigorously administered.
The Newton settlers were joined by Quakers from
Long Island, where, under the English law as
administered by the New York governors, they
had also been fined and imprisoned, though with
less severity than at home, for nonconformity
to the Church of England.   On arriving, the
West Jersey settlers suffered some hardships during the year that must elapse before a crop could
be raised and a log cabin or house built.   During
that period they usually lived, in the Indian manner, in wigwams of poles covered with bark, or in
caves protected with logs in the steep banks of
the creeks.   Many of them lived in the villages
of the Indians.   The Indians supplied them all
with corn and venison, and without this Indian
help, they would have run serious risk of starving,
for they were not accustomed to hunting.   They
had also to thank the Indians for having in past
ages removed so much of the heavy forest growth
from the wide strip of land along the river that
it was easy to start cultivation.

These Quaker settlers made a point of dealing
very justly with the Indians and the two races
lived side by side for several generations.   There
is an instance recorded of the Indians attending

with much solemnity the funeral of a prominent Quaker woman, Esther Spicer, for whom they had acquired great respect. The funeral was held at night, and the Indians in canoes, the white men in boats, passed down Cooper's Creek and along the river to Newton Creek where the graveyard was, lighting the darkness with innumerable torches, a strange scene to think of now as having been once enacted in front of the bustling cities of Camden and Philadelphia. Some of the young settlers took Indian wives, and that strain of native blood is said to show itself in the features of several families to this day.

Many letters of these settlers have been preserved, all expressing the greatest enthusiasm for the new country, for the splendid river better than the Thames, the good climate, and their improved health, the immense relief to be away from the constant dread of fines and punishment, the chance to rise in the world, with large rewards for industry. They note the immense quantities of game, the Indians bringing in fat bucks every day, the venison better than in England, the streams full of fish, the abundance of wild fruits, cranberries, hurtleberries, the rapid increase of cattle, and the good soil.

A few details concerning some of the interesting characters among these early colonial Quakers have been rescued from oblivion. There is, for instance, the pleasing picture of a young man and his sister, convinced Quakers, coming out together and pioneering in their log cabin until each found a partner for life. There was John Haddon, from whom Haddonfield is named, who bought a large tract of land but remained in England, while his daughter Elizabeth came out alone to look after it. A strong, decisive character she was, and women of that sort have always been encouraged in independent action by the Quakers. She proved to be an excellent manager of an estate. The romance of her marriage to a young Quaker preacher, Estaugh, has been celebrated in Mrs. Maria Child's novel *The Youthful Emigrant*. The pair became leading citizens devoted to good works and to Quaker liberalism for many a year in Haddonfield.

It was the ship *Shields of Hull*, bringing Quaker immigrants to Burlington, of which the story is told that in beating up the river she tacked close to the rather high bank with deep water frontage where Philadelphia was afterwards established; and some of the passengers remarked that it was a fine site for a town. The *Shields*, it is said, was the first ship to sail up as far as Burlington. Anchoring before Burlington in the evening, the colonists woke up next morning to find the river frozen hard so that they walked on the ice to their future habitations.

Burlington was made the capital of West Jersey, a legislature was convened and laws were passed under the "concessions" or constitution of the proprietors. Salem and Burlington became the ports of the little province, which was well under way by 1682, when Penn came out to take possession of Pennsylvania.

The West Jersey people of these two settlements spread eastward into the interior but were stopped by a great forest area known as the Pines, or Pine Barrens, of such heavy growth that even the Indians lived on its outer edges and entered it only for hunting. It was an irregularly shaped tract, full of wolves, bear, beaver, deer, and other game, and until recent years continued to attract sportsmen from all parts of the country. Starting near Delaware Bay, it extended parallel with the ocean as far north as the lower portion of the present Monmouth County and formed a region about seventy-five miles long and thirty miles wide. It was roughly the part of the old sandy shoal that first emerged from the ocean, and it has been longer above water than any other part of southern Jersey. The old name, Pine Barrens, is hardly correct because it implies something like a desert, when as a matter of fact the region produced magnificent forest trees.

The innumerable visitors who cross southern Jersey to the famous seashore resorts always pass through the remains of this old central forest and are likely to conclude that the monotonous low scrub oaks and stunted pines on sandy level soil, seen for the last two or three generations, were always there and that the primeval forest of colonial times was no better. But that is a mistake. The stunted growth now seen is not even second growth but in many cases fourth or fifth or more. The whole region was cut over long ago. The original growth, pine in many places, consisted also of lofty timber of oak, hickory, gum, ash, chestnut, and numerous other trees, interspersed with dogwood, sassafras, and holly, and in the swamps the beautiful magnolia, along with the valuable white cedar. De Vries, who visited the Jersey coast about 1632, at what is supposed to have been Beesley's or Somer's Point, describes high woods coming down to the shore. Even to-day, immediately back of Somer's Point, there is a magnificent lofty oak forest accidentally preserved by surrounding marsh from the destructive forest fires; and there are similar groves along the road towards Pleasantville. In fact, the finest forest trees flourish in that region wherever given a good chance. Even some of the beaches of Cape May had valuable oak and luxuriant growths of red cedar; and until a few years ago there were fine trees, especially hollies, surviving on Wildwood Beach.

The Jersey white cedar swamps were, and still are, places of fascinating interest to the naturalist and the botanist. The hunter or explorer found them scattered almost everywhere in the old forest and near its edges, varying in size from a few square yards up to hundreds of acres. They were formed by little streams easily checked in their flow through the level land by decaying vegetation or dammed by beavers. They kept the water within the country, preventing all effects of droughts, stimulating the growth of vegetation which by its decay, throughout the centuries, was steadily adding vegetable mold or humus to the sandy soil. This process of building up a richer soil has now been largely stopped by lumbering, drainage, and fires.

While there are many of these swamps left, the appearance of numbers of them has largely changed. When the white men first came, the great cedars three or four feet in diameter which had fallen centuries before often lay among the living trees, some of them buried deep in the mud and preserved from decay. They were invaluable timber, and digging them out and cutting them up became an important industry for over a hundred years. In addition to being used for boat building, they made excellent shingles which would last a lifetime. The swamps, indeed, became known as shingle mines, and it was a good description of them. An important trade was developed in hogshead staves, hoops, shingles, boards, and planks, much of which went into the West Indian trade to be exchanged for rum, sugar, molasses, and negroes.[1]

---

[1] "Between the years 1740 and '50, the Cedar Swamps of the county [Cape May] were mostly located; and the amount of lumber since taken from them is incalculable, not only as an article of trade, but to supply the home demand for fencing and building material in the county. Large portions of these swamps have been worked a second and some a third time, since located. At the present time [1857] there is not an acre of original growth of swamp standing, having all passed away before the resistless sway of the speculator or the consumer." Beesley's *Sketch of Cape May*, p. 197.

The great forest has long since been lumbered to death. The pines were worked for tar, pitch, resin, and turpentine until for lack of material the industry passed southward through the Carolinas to Florida, exhausting the trees as it went. The Christmas demand for holly has almost stripped the Jersey woods of these trees once so numerous. Destructive fires and frequent cutting keep the pine and oak lands stunted. Thousands of dollars' worth of cedar springing up in the swamps are sometimes destroyed in a day. But efforts to control the fires so destructive not only to this standing timber but to the fertility of the soil, and attempts to reforest this country not only for the sake of timber but as an attraction to those who resort there in search of health or natural beauty, have not been vigorously pushed. The great forest has now, to be sure, been partially cultivated in spots, and the sand used for large glass-making industries. Small fruits and grapes flourish in some places. At the northern end of this forest tract the health resort known as Lakewood was established to take advantage of the pine air. A little to the southward is the secluded Brown's Mills, once so appealing to lovers of the simple life.

Checked on the east by the great forest, the West Jersey Quakers spread southward from Salem until they came to the Cohansey, a large and beautiful stream flowing out of the forest and wandering through green meadows and marshes to the bay. So numerous were the wild geese along its shores and along the Maurice River farther south that the first settlers are said to have killed them for their feathers alone and to have thrown the carcasses away. At the head of navigation of the Cohansey was a village called Cohansey Bridge, and after 1765 Bridgeton, a name still borne by a flourishing modern town. Lower down near the marsh was the village of Greenwich, the principal place of business up to the year 1800, with a foreign trade. Some of the tea the East India Company tried to force on the colonists during the Revolution was sent there and was duly rejected. It is still an extremely pretty village, with its broad shaded streets like a New England town and its old Quaker meeting house. In fact, not a few New Englanders from Connecticut, still infatuated with southern Jersey in spite of the rebuffs received in ancient times from Dutch and Swedes, finally settled near the Cohansey after it came under control of the more amiable Quakers. There

was also one place called after Fairfield in Connecticut and another called New England Town.

The first churches of this region were usually
built near running streams so that the congregation could procure water for themselves and their
horses.   Of one old Presbyterian Church it used to
be said that no one had ever ridden to it in a wheeled
vehicle.   Wagons and carriages were very scarce
until after the Revolution.   Carts for occasions
of ceremony as well as utility were used before
wagons and carriages.   For a hundred and fifty
years the horse's back was the best form of conveyance in the deep sand of the trails and roads.
This was true of all southern Jersey.   Pack horses
and the backs of Indian and negro slaves were
the principal means of transportation on land.
The roads and trails, in fact, were so few and so
heavy with sand that water travel was very much
developed.   The Indian dugout canoe was adopted
and found faster and better than heavy English
rowboats.   As the province was almost surrounded
by water and was covered with a network of creeks
and channels, nearly all the villages and towns were
situated on tidewater streams, and the dugout canoe, modified and improved, was for several generations the principal means of communication.

Most of the old roads in New Jersey followed Indian trails. There was a trail, for example, from the modern Camden opposite Philadelphia, following up Cooper's Creek past Berlin, then called Long-a-coming, crossing the watershed, and then following Great Egg Harbor River to the seashore. Another trail, long used by the settlers, led from Salem up to Camden, Burlington, and Trenton, going round the heads of streams. It was afterwards abandoned for the shorter route obtained by bridging the streams nearer their mouths. This old trail also extended from the neighborhood of Trenton to Perth Amboy near the mouth of the Hudson, and thus, by supplementing the lower routes, made a trail nearly the whole length of the province.

As a Quaker refuge, West Jersey never attained the success of Pennsylvania. The political disturbances and the continually threatened loss of self-government in both the Jerseys were a serious deterrent to Quakers who, above all else, prized rights which they found far better secured in Pennsylvania. In 1702, when the two Jerseys were united into one colony under a government appointed by the Crown, those rights were more restricted than ever and all hopes of West Jersey becoming a colony under complete Quaker control were shattered. Under Governor Cornbury, the English law was adopted and enforced, and the Quakers were disqualified from testifying in court unless they took an oath and were prohibited from serving on juries or holding any office of trust. Cornbury's judges wore scarlet robes, powdered wigs, cocked hats, gold lace, and side arms; they were conducted to the courthouse by the sheriff's cavalcade and opened court with great parade and ceremony. Such a spectacle of pomp was sufficient to divert the flow of Quaker immigrants to Pennsylvania, where the government was entirely in Quaker hands and where plain and serious ways gave promise of enduring and unmolested prosperity.

The Quakers had altogether thirty meeting houses in West Jersey and eleven in East Jersey, which probably shows about the proportion of Quaker influence in the two Jerseys. Many of them have since disappeared; some of the early buildings, to judge from the pictures, were of wood and not particularly pleasing in appearance. They were makeshifts, usually intended to be replaced by better buildings. Some substantial brick buildings of excellent architecture have survived, and their plainness and simplicity, combined with excellent proportions and thorough construction, are clearly indicative of Quaker character. There is a particularly interesting one in Salem with a magnificent old oak beside it, another in the village of Greenwich on the Cohansey farther south, and another at Crosswicks near Trenton.

In West Jersey near Mount Holly was born and lived John Woolman, a Quaker who became eminent throughout the English speaking world for the simplicity and loftiness of his religious thought as well as for his admirable style of expression. His *Journal*, once greatly and even extravagantly admired, still finds readers. "Get the writings of John Woolman by heart," said Charles Lamb, "and love the early Quakers." He was among the Quakers one of the first and perhaps the first really earnest advocate of the abolition of slavery. The scenes of West Jersey and the writings of Woolman seem to belong together. Possibly a feeling for the simplicity of those scenes and their life led Walt Whitman, who grew up on Long Island under Quaker influence, to spend his last years at Camden, in West Jersey. His profound democracy, which was very Quaker-like, was more at home there perhaps than anywhere else.

CHAPTER IX

Most of the colonies in America, especially the stronger ones, had an aristocratic class, which was often large and powerful, as in the case of Virginia, and which usually centered around the governor, especially if he were appointed from England by the Crown or by a proprietor. But there was very little of this social distinction in New Jersey. Her political life had been too much broken up, and she had been too long dependent on the governors of New York to have any of those pretty little aristocracies with bright colored clothes, and coaches and four, flourishing within her boundaries. There seems to have been a faint suggestion of such social pretensions under Governor Franklin just before the Revolution. He was beginning to live down the objections to his illegitimate birth and Toryism and by his entertainments and manner of living was creating a social

following.   There is said also to have been something a little like the beginning of an aristocracy
among the descendants of the Dutch settlers who
had ancestral holdings near the Hudson; but this
amounted to very little.

Class distinctions were not so strongly marked
in New Jersey as in some other colonies. There
grew up in southern Jersey, however, a sort of
aristocracy of gentlemen farmers, who owned
large tracts of land and lived in not a little style
in good houses on the small streams.

The northern part of the province, largely settled
and influenced by New Englanders, was like New
England a land of vigorous concentrated town life
and small farms. The hilly and mountainous nature
of the northern section naturally led to small holdings of land. But in southern Jersey the level sandy
tracts of forest were often taken up in large areas.
In the absence of manufacturing, large acreage
naturally became, as in Virginia and Maryland,
the only mark of wealth and social distinction.
The great landlord was looked up to by the lesser
fry. The Quaker rule of discountenancing marry-
ing out of meeting tended to keep a large acreage
in the family and to make it larger by marriage.
A Quaker of broad acres would seek for his daughter

a young man of another landholding Quaker family and would thus join the two estates.

There was a marked difference between East Jersey and West Jersey in county organization. In West Jersey the people tended to become planters; their farms and plantations somewhat like those of the far South; and the political unit of government was the county. In East Jersey the town was the starting point and the county marked the boundaries of a collection of towns. This curious difference, the result of soil, climate, and methods of life, shows itself in other States wherever South and North meet. Illinois is an example, where the southern part of the State is governed by the county system, and the northern part by the town system.

The lumberman, too, in clearing off the primeval forest and selling the timber, usually dealt in immense acreage. Some families, it is said, can be traced steadily proceeding southward as they stripped off the forest, and started sawmills and gristmills on the little streams that trickled from the swamps, and like beavers making with their dams those pretty ponds which modern lovers of the picturesque are now so eager to find. A good deal of the lumbering in the interior pines tract was carried on by persons who leased the premises from owners who lived on plantations along the Delaware or its tributary streams. These operations began soon after 1700. Wood roads were cut into the Pines, sawmills were started, and constant use turned some of these wood roads into the highways of modern times.

There was a speculative tinge in the operations of this landed aristocracy. Like the old tobacco raising aristocracy of Virginia and Maryland, they were inclined to go from tract to tract, skinning what they could from a piece of deforested land and then seeking another virgin tract. The roughest methods were used; wooden plows, brush harrows, straw collars, grapevine harness, and poor shelter for animals and crops; but were the Virginia methods any better? In these operations there was apparently a good deal of sudden profit and mushroom prosperity accompanied by a good deal of debt and insolvency. In this, too, they were like the Virginians and Carolinians. There seem to have been also a good many slaves in West Jersey, brought, as in the southern colonies, to work on the large estates, and this also, no doubt, helped to foster the aristocratic feeling.

The best days of the Jersey gentlemen farmers

came probably when they could no longer move
from tract to tract. They settled down and enjoyed
a very plentiful, if rude, existence on the products
of their land, game, and fish, amid a fine climate
— with mosquitoes enough in summer to act as
a counterirritant and prevent stagnation from too
much ease and prosperity. After the manner of
colonial times, they wove their own clothes from
the wool of their own sheep and made their own
implements, furniture, and simple machinery.
There are still to be found fascinating traces of
this old life in out-of-the-way parts of southern
Jersey. To run upon old houses among the Jersey
pines still stored with Latin classics and old edi-
tions of Shakespeare, Addison, or Samuel Johnson, to come across an old mill with its machinery, cogwheels, flywheels, and all, made of wood,
to find people who make their own oars, and the
handles of their tools from the materials furnished by their own forest, is now unfortunately
a refreshment of the spirit that is daily becoming
rarer.

This condition of material and social self-suffi-
ciency lasted in places long after the Revolution.
It was a curious little aristocracy — a very faint
and faded one, lacking the robustness of the far

southern type, and lacking indeed the real essential of an aristocracy, namely political power. Moreover, although there were slaves in New Jersey, there were not enough of them to exalt the Jersey gentlemen farmers into such self-sufficient lords and masters as the Virginian and Carolinian planters became.

To search out the remains of this stage of American history, however, takes one up many pleasant streams flowing out of the forest tract to the Delaware on one side or to the ocean on the other. This topographical formation of a central ridge or watershed of forest and swamp was a repetition of the same formation in the Delaware peninsula, which like southern Jersey had originally been a shoal and then an island. The Jersey watershed, with its streams abounding in wood duck and all manner of wild life, must have been in its primeval days as fascinating as some of the streams of the Florida cypress swamps. Toward the ocean, Wading River, the Mullica, the Tuckahoe, Great Egg; and on the Delaware side the Maurice, Cohansey, Salem Creek, Oldman's, Raccoon, Mantua, Woodberry, Timber, and the Rancocas, still possess attraction. Some of them, on opposite sides of the divide, are not far apart at their

sources in the old forest tract; so that a canoe can
be transported over the few miles and thus traverse
the State.   One of these trips up Timber Creek
from the Delaware and across only eight miles of
land to the headwaters of Great Egg Harbor
River and thence down to the ocean, thus cutting
South Jersey in half, is a particularly romantic
one.   The heavy woods and swamps of this secluded route along these forest shadowed streams
are apparently very much as they were three hundred years ago.

The water in all these streams, particularly in
their upper parts, owing to the sandy soil, is very
clean and clear and is often stained by the cedar
roots in the swamps a clear brown, sometimes
almost an amber color.   One of the streams, the
Rancocas, with its many windings to Mount Holly
and then far inland to Brown's Mills, seems to
be the favorite with canoemen and is probably
without an equal in its way for those who love
the Indian's gift that brings us so close to nature.

The spread of the Quaker settlements along
Delaware Bay to Cape May was checked by the
Maurice River and its marshes and by the Great
Cedar Swamp which crossed the country from

Delaware Bay to the ocean and thus made of the Cape May region a sort of island. The Cape May region, it is true, was settled by Quakers, but most of them came from Long Island rather than from the settlements on the Delaware. They had followed whale fishing on Long Island and in pursuit of that occupation some of them had migrated to Cape May where whales were numerous not far off shore.

The leading early families of Cape May, the Townsends, Stillwells, Corsons, Leamings, Ludlams, Spicers, and Cresses, many of whose descendants still live there, were Quakers of the Long Island strain. The ancestor of the Townsend family came to Cape May because he had been imprisoned and fined and threatened with worse under the New York government for assisting his fellow Quakers to hold meetings. Probably the occasional severity of the administration of the New York laws against Quakers, which were the same as those of England, had as much to do as had the whales with the migration to Cape May. This Quaker civilization extended from Cape May up as far as Great Egg Harbor where the Great Cedar Swamp joined the seashore. Quaker meeting houses were built at Cape May, Galloway,

Tuckahoe, and Great Egg. All have been abandoned and the buildings themselves have disappeared, except that of the Cape May meeting, called the Old Cedar Meeting, at Seaville; and it has no congregation. The building is kept in repair by members of the Society from other places.

Besides the Quakers, Cape May included a number of New Haven people, the first of whom came there as early as 1640 under the leadership of George Lamberton and Captain Turner, seeking profit in whale fishing. They were not driven out by the Dutch and Swedes, as happened to their companions who attempted to settle higher up the river at Salem and the Schuylkill. About one-fifth of the old family names of Cape May and New Haven are similar, and there is supposed to be not a little New England blood not only in Cape May but in the neighboring counties of Cumberland and Salem. While the first New Haven whalers came to Cape May in 1640, it is probable that for a long time they only sheltered their vessels there, and none of them became permanent settlers until about 1685.

Scandinavians contributed another element to the population of the Cape May region. Very little is definitely known about this settlement,.

but the Swedish names in Cape May and Cumberland counties seem to indicate a migration of Scandinavians from Wilmington and Tinicum.

Great Egg Harbor, which formed the northern part of the Cape May settlement, was named from the immense numbers of wild fowl, swans, ducks, and water birds that formerly nested there every summer and have now been driven to Canada or beyond. Little Egg Harbor farther up the coast was named for the same reason as well as Egg Island, of three hundred acres in Delaware Bay, since then eaten away by the tide. The people of the district had excellent living from the eggs as well as from the plentiful fowl, fish, and oysters.

Some farming was done by the inhabitants of Cape May; and many cattle, marked with brands but in a half wild state, were kept out on the uninhabited beaches which have now become seaside summer cities. Some of the cattle were still running wild on the beaches down to the time of the Civil War. The settlers "mined" the valuable white cedar from the swamps for shingles and boards, leaving great "pool holes" in the swamps which even today sometimes trap the unwary sportsman. The women knitted innumerable mittens and also made wampum or Indian money from the clam and oyster shells, an important means of exchange in the Indian trade all over the colonies, and even to some extent among the colonists themselves. The Cape May people built sloops for carrying the white cedar, the mittens, oysters, and wampum to the outside world. They sold a great deal of their cedar in Long Island, Rhode Island, and Connecticut. Philadelphia finally became their market for oysters and also for lumber, corn, and the whalebone and oil. Their sloops also traded to the southern colonies and even to the West Indies.

They were an interesting little community, these Cape May people, very isolated and dependent on the water and on their boats, for they were completely cut off by the Great Cedar Swamp which stretched across the point and separated them from the rest of the coast. This troublesome swamp was not bridged for many years; and even then the roads to it were long, slow, and too sandy for transporting anything of much bulk.

Next above Cape May on the coast was another isolated patch of civilization which, while not an island, was nevertheless cut off on the south by Great Egg Harbor with its river and marshes, and on the north by Little Egg Harbor with the Mullica River and its marshes extending far inland. The people in this district also lived somewhat to themselves. To the north lay the district which extended to Sandy Hook, also with its distinct set of people.

The people of the Cape became in colonial times clever traders in various pursuits. Although in one sense they were as isolated as islanders, their adventurous life on the sea gave them breadth of view. By their thrift and in innumerable shrewd and persistent ways they amassed competencies and estates for their families. Aaron Leaming, for example, who died in 1780, left an estate of nearly $1,000,000. Some kept diaries which have become historically valuable in showing not only their history but their good education and the peculiar cast of their mind for keen trading as well as their rigid economy and integrity.

One character, Jacob Spicer, a prosperous colonial, insisted on having everything made at home by his sons and daughters — shoes, clothes, leather breeches, wampum, even shoe thread — calculating the cost of everything to a fraction and economizing to the last penny of money and the last second of time. Yet in the course of a year he used "fifty-two gallons of rum, ten of wine, and two barrels of cyder." Apparently in those days hard labor and hard drinking went well together.

The Cape May people, relying almost entirely on the water for communication and trade, soon took to piloting vessels in the Delaware River, and some of them still follow this occupation. They also became skillful sailors and builders of small craft, and it is not surprising to learn that Jacocks Swain and his sons introduced, in 1811, the centerboard for keeping flat-bottomed craft closer to the wind. They are said to have taken out a patent for this invention and are given the credit of being the originators of the idea. But the device was known in England in 1774, was introduced in Massachusetts in the same year, and may have been used long before by the Dutch. The need of it, however, was no doubt strongly impressed upon the Cape May people by the difficulties which their little sloops experienced in beating home against contrary winds. Some of them, indeed, spent weeks in sight of the Cape, unable to make it. One sloop, the *Nancy*, seventy-two days from Demarara, hung off and on for forty-three days from December 25, 1787, to February 6, 1788, and was driven off fifteen times before she finally got into Hereford Inlet. Sometimes better sailing craft had to go out and bring in such distressed vessels. The early boats were no doubt badly constructed; but in the end apprenticeship to dire necessity made the Cape May sailors masters of seamanship and the windward art.[1]

Wilson, the naturalist, spent a great deal of time in the Cape May region, because of the great variety of birds to be found there. Southern types, like the Florida egret, ventured even so far north, and it was a stopping place for migrating birds, notably woodcock, on their northern and southern journeys. Men of the stone age had once been numerous in this region, as the remains of village plats and great shell heaps bore witness. It was a resting point for all forms of life. That much traveled, adventurous gentleman of the sea, Captain Kidd, according to popular legend, was a frequent visitor to this coast.

In later times, beginning in 1801, the Cape became one of the earliest of the summer resorts. The famous Commodore Decatur was among the first distinguished men to be attracted by the simple seaside charm of the place, long before it was destroyed by wealth and crowds. Year by

[1] Stevens, *History of Cape May County*, pp. 219, 229; Kelley, *American Yachts* (1884), p. 165.

year he used to measure and record at one spot the encroachment of the sea upon the beach. Where today the sea washes and the steel pier extends, once lay cornfields. For a hundred years it was a favorite resting place for statesmen and politicians of national eminence. They traveled there by stage, sailing sloop, or their own wagons. People from Baltimore and the South more particularly sought the place because it was easily accessible from the head of Chesapeake Bay by an old railroad, long since abandoned, to New Castle on the Delaware, whence sail- or steamboats went to Cape May. This avoided the tedious stage ride over the sandy Jersey roads. Presidents, cabinet officers, senators, and congressmen sought the invigorating air of the Cape and the attractions of the old village, its seafaring life, the sailing, fishing, and bathing on the best beach of the coast. Congress Hall, their favorite hotel, became famous, and during a large part of the nineteenth century presidential nominations and policies are said to have been planned within its walls.

CHAPTER X

SCOTCH COVENANTERS AND OTHERS IN EAST JERSEY

EAST JERSEY was totally different in its topography from West Jersey. The northern half of the State is a region of mountains and lakes. As part of the original continent it had been under the ice sheet of the glacial age and was very unlike the level sands, swamps, and pine barrens of West Jersey which had arisen as a shoal and island from the sea. The only place in East Jersey where settlement was at all easy was along the open meadows which were reached by water near the mouth of the Hudson, round Newark Bay, and along the Hackensack River.

The Dutch, by the discoveries of Henry Hudson in 1609, claimed the whole region between the Hudson and the Delaware. They settled part of East Jersey opposite their headquarters at New York and called it Pavonia. But their cruel massacre of some Indians who sought refuge among them at Pavonia destroyed the prospects of the settlement. The Indians revenged themselves by massacring the Dutch again and again, every time they attempted to reëstablish Pavonia. This kept the Dutch out of East Jersey until 1660, when they succeeded in establishing Bergen between Newark Bay and the Hudson.

The Dutch authority in America was overthrown in 1664 by Charles II, who had already given all New Jersey to his brother the Duke of York. Colonel Richard Nicolls commanded the British expedition that seized the Dutch possessions; and he had been given full power as deputy governor of all the Duke of York's vast territory.

Meantime the New England Puritans seem to have kept their eyes on East Jersey as a desirable region, and the moment the Connecticut Puritans heard of Nicolls' appointment, they applied to him for a grant of a large tract of land on Newark Bay. In the next year, 1665, he gave them another tract from the mouth of the Raritan to Sandy Hook; and soon the villages of Shrewsbury and Middletown were started.

Meantime, however, unknown to Nicolls, the Duke of York in England had given all of New Jersey to Lord Berkeley and Sir George Carteret.

As has already been pointed out, they had divided the province between them, and East Jersey had fallen to Carteret, who sent out, with some immigrants, his relative Philip Carteret as governor. Governor Carteret was of course very much surprised to find so much of the best land already occupied by the excellent and thrifty Yankees. As a consequence, litigation and sometimes civil war over this unlucky mistake lasted for a hundred years. Many of the Yankee settlers under the Nicolls grant refused to pay quitrents to Carteret or his successors and, in spite of a commission of inquiry from England in 1751 and a chancery suit, they held their own until the Revolution of 1776 extinguished all British authority.

There was therefore from the beginning a strong New England tinge in East Jersey which has lasted to this day. Governor Carteret established a village on Newark Bay which still bears the name Elizabeth, which he gave it in honor of the wife of the proprietor, and he made it the capital. There were also immigrants from Scotland and England. But Puritans from Long Island and New England continued to settle round Newark Bay. By virtue either of character or numbers, New Englanders were evidently the controlling element, for they established the New England system of town government, and imposed strict Connecticut laws, making twelve crimes punishable with death. Soon there were flourishing little villages, Newark and Elizabeth, besides Middletown and Shrewsbury. The next year Piscataway and Woodbridge were added. Newark and the region round it, including the Oranges, was settled by very exclusive Puritans, or Congregationalists, as they are now called, some thirty families from four Connecticut towns — Milford, Guilford, Bradford, and New Haven. They decided that only church members should hold office and vote.

Governor Carteret ruled the colony with an appointive council and a general assembly elected by the people, the typical colonial form of government. His administration lasted from 1665 to his death in 1682; and there is nothing very remarkable to record except the rebellion of the New Englanders, especially those who had received their land from Nicolls. Such independent Connecticut people were, of course, quite out of place in a proprietary colony, and, when in 1670 the first collection of quitrents was attempted, they broke out in violent opposition, in which the settlers of Elizabeth were prominent. In 1672 they elected a revolutionary assembly of their own and, in place of the deputy governor, appointed as proprietor a natural son of Carteret. They began imprisoning former officers and confiscating estates in the most approved revolutionary form and for a time had the whole government in their control. It required the interference of the Duke of York, of the proprietors, and of the British Crown to allay the little tempest, and three years were given in which to pay the quitrents.

After the death of Sir George Carteret in 1680, his province of East Jersey was sold to William Penn and eleven other Quakers for the sum of £3400. Colonies seem to have been comparatively inexpensive luxuries in those days. A few years before, in 1675, Penn and some other Quakers had, as has already been related, gained control of West Jersey for the still smaller sum of one thousand pounds and had established it as a Quaker refuge. It might be supposed that they now had the same purpose in view in East Jersey, but apparently their intention was to create a refuge for Presbyterians, the famous Scotch Covenanters, much persecuted at that time under Charles II, who was forcing them to conform to the Church of England.

Penn and his fellow proprietors of East Jersey each chose a partner, most of them Scotchmen, two of whom, the Earl of Perth and Lord Drummond, were prominent men. To this mixed body of Quakers, other dissenters, and some Papists, twenty-four proprietors in all, the Duke of York reconfirmed by special patent their right to East Jersey. Under their urging a few Scotch Covenanters began to arrive and seem to have first established themselves at Perth Amboy, which they named from the Scottish Earl of Perth and an Indian word meaning "point." This settlement they expected to become a great commercial port rivaling New York. Curiously enough, Robert Barclay, the first governor appointed, was not only a Scotchman but also a Quaker, and a theologian whose *Apology for the True Christian Divinity* (1678) is regarded to this day as the best statement of the original Quaker doctrine. He remained in England, however, and the deputies whom he sent out to rule the colony had a troublous time of it.

That Quakers should establish a refuge for Presbyterians seems at first peculiar, but it was in accord with their general philanthropic plan to help the oppressed and suffering, to rescue prisoners and exiles, and especially to ameliorate the horrible condition of people confined in the English dungeons and prisons. Many vivid pictures of how the Scotch Covenanters were hunted down like wild beasts may be found in English histories and novels. When their lives were spared they often met a fate worse than death in the loathsome dungeons into which thousands of Quakers of that time were also thrust. A large part of William Penn's life as a courtier was spent in rescuing prisoners, exiles, and condemned persons of all sorts, and not merely those of his own faith. So the undertaking to make of Jersey two colonies, one a refuge for Quakers and the other a refuge for Covenanters, was natural enough, and it was a very broad-minded plan for that age.

In 1683, a few years after the Quaker control of East Jersey began, a new and fiercer persecution of the Covenanters was started in the old country, and shortly afterwards Monmouth's insurrection in England broke out and was followed by a most bloody proscription and punishment. The greatest efforts were made to induce those still untouched to fly for refuge to East Jersey; but, strange to say, comparatively few of them came. It is another proof of the sturdiness and devotion which has filled so many pages of history and romance with their praise that as a class the Covenanters remained at home to establish their faith with torture, martyrdom, and death.

In 1685 the Duke of York ascended the throne of England as James II, and all that was naturally to be expected from such a bigoted despot was soon realized. The persecutions of the Covenanters grew worse. Crowded into prisons to die of thirst and suffocation, shot down on the highways, tied to stakes to be drowned by the rising tide, the whole Calvinistic population of Scotland seemed doomed to extermination. Again they were told of America as the only place where religious liberty was allowed, and in addition a book was circulated among them called *The Model of the Government of the Province of East Jersey in America*. These efforts were partially successful. More Covenanters came than before, but nothing like the numbers of Quakers that flocked to Pennsylvania. The whole population of East Jersey — New Englanders, Dutch, Scotch Covenanters, and all — did not exceed five thousand and possibly was not over four thousand.

Some French Huguenots, such as came to many of the English colonies after the Revocation of the Edict of Nantes of 1685, were added to the East

Jersey population. A few went to Salem in West Jersey, and some of these became Quakers. In both the Jerseys, as elsewhere, they became prominent and influential in all spheres of life. There was a decided Dutch influence, it is said, in the part nearest New York, emanating from the Bergen settlement in which the Dutch had succeeded in establishing themselves in 1660 after the Indians had twice driven them from Pavonia. Many descendants of Dutch families are still found in that region. Many Dutch characteristics were to be found in that region throughout colonial times. Many of the houses had Dutch stoops or porches at the door, with seats where the family and visitors sat on summer evenings to smoke and gossip. Long Dutch spouts extended out from the eaves to discharge the rain water into the street. But the prevailing tone of East Jersey seems to have been set by the Scotch Presbyterians and the New England Congregationalists. The College of New Jersey, afterward known as Princeton, established in 1747, was the result of a movement among the Presbyterians of East Jersey and New York.

All these elements of East Jersey, Scotch Covenanters, Connecticut Puritans, Huguenots, and

Dutch of the Dutch Reformed Church, were in a sense different but in reality very much in accord and congenial in their ideas of religion and politics. They were all sturdy, freedom-loving Protestants, and they set the tone that prevails in East Jersey to this day. Their strict discipline and their uncompromising thrift may now seem narrow and harsh; but it made them what they were; and it has left a legacy of order and prosperity under which alien religions and races are eager to seek protection. In its foundation the Quakers may claim a share.

The new King, James II, was inclined to reassume jurisdiction and extend the power of the Governor of New York over East Jersey in spite of his grant to Sir George Carteret. In fact, he desired to put New England, New York, and New Jersey under one strong government centered at New York, to abolish their charters, to extinguish popular government, and to make them all mere royal dependencies in pursuance of his general policy of establishing an absolute monarchy and a papal church in England.

The curse of East Jersey's existence was to be always an appendage of New York, or to be threatened with that condition. The inhabitants now

had to enter their vessels and pay duties at New
York. Writs were issued by order of the King
putting both the Jerseys and all New England under the New York Governor. Step by step the
plans for amalgamation and despotism moved on
successfully, when suddenly the English Revolution
of 1688 put an end to the whole magnificent scheme,
drove the King into exile, and placed William of
Orange on the throne.

The proprietaries of both Jerseys reassumed
their former authority. But the New York Assembly attempted to exercise control over East
Jersey and to levy duties on its exports. The
two provinces were soon on the eve of a little
war. For twelve or fifteen years East Jersey was
in disorder, with seditious meetings, mob rule,
judges and sheriffs attacked while performing
their duty, the proprietors claiming quitrents
from the people, the people resisting, and the
British Privy Council threatening a suit to take
the province from the proprietors and make a
Crown colony of it. The period is known in the
history of this colony as "The Revolution." Under the threat of the Privy Council to take over
the province, the proprietors of both East and
West Jersey surrendered their rights of political

government, retaining their ownership of land and quitrents, and the two Jerseys were united under one government in 1702. Its subsequent history demands another chapter.

CHAPTER XI

THE UNITED JERSEYS

THE Quaker colonists grouped round Burlington and Salem, on the Delaware, and the Scotch Covenanters and New England colonists grouped around Perth Amboy and Newark, near the mouth of the Hudson, made up the two Jerseys. Neither colony had a numerous population, and the stretch of country lying between them was during most of the colonial period a wilderness. It is now crossed by the railway from Trenton to New York. It has always been a line of travel from the Delaware to the Hudson. At first there was only an Indian trail across it, but after 1695 there was a road, and after 1738 a stage route.

In 1702, while still separated by this wilderness, the two Jerseys were united politically by the proprietors voluntarily surrendering all their political rights to the Crown. The political distinction between East Jersey and West Jersey was thus

abolished; their excellent free constitutions were
rendered of doubtful authority; and from that
time to the Revolution they constituted one colony
under the control of a royal governor appointed
by the Crown.

The change was due to the uncertainty and an-
noyance caused for their separate governments
when their right to govern was in doubt owing to
interference on the part of New York and the
desire of the King to make them a Crown colony.
The original grant of the Duke of York to the
proprietors Berkeley and Carteret had given title
to the soil but had been silent as to the right to
govern. The first proprietors and their successors
had always assumed that the right to govern
necessarily accompanied this gift of the land. Such
a privilege, however, the Crown was inclined to
doubt. William Penn was careful to avoid this
uncertainty when he received his charter for Pennsylvania. Profiting by the sad example of the
Jerseys, he made sure that he was given both the
title to the soil and the right to govern.

The proprietors, however, now surrendered only
their right to govern the Jerseys and retained their
ownership of the land; and the people always
maintained that they, on their part, retained all

the political rights and privileges which had been granted them by the proprietors. And these rights were important, for the concessions or constitutions granted by the proprietors under the advanced Quaker influence of the time were decidedly liberal. The assemblies, as the legislatures were called, had the right to meet and adjourn as they pleased, instead of having their meetings and adjournments dictated by the governor. This was an important right and one which the Crown and royal governors were always trying to restrict or destroy, because it made an assembly very independent. This contest for colonial rights was exactly similar to the struggle of the English Parliament for liberty against the supposed right of the Stuart kings to call and adjourn Parliament as they chose. If the governor could adjourn the assembly when he pleased, he could force it to pass any laws he wanted or prevent its passing any laws at all. The two Jersey assemblies under their Quaker constitutions also had the privilege of making their own rules of procedure, and they had jurisdiction over taxes, roads, towns, militia, and all details of government. These rights of a legislature are familiar enough now to all. Very few people realize, however, what a struggle and what sacrifices were required to attain them.

The rest of New Jersey colonial history is made up chiefly of struggles over these two questions — the rights of the proprietors and their quitrents as against the people, and the rights of the new assembly as against the Crown. There were thus three parties, the governor and his adherents, the proprietors and their friends, and the assembly and the people. The proprietors had the best of the change, for they lost only their troublesome political power and retained their property. They never, however, received such financial returns from the property as the sons of William Penn enjoyed from Pennsylvania. But the union of the Jerseys seriously curtailed the rights enjoyed by the people under the old government, and all possibility of a Quaker government in West Jersey was ended. It was this experience in the Jerseys, no doubt, that caused William Penn to require so many safeguards in selling his political rights in Pennsylvania to the Crown that the sale was, fortunately for the colony, never completed.

The assembly under the union met alternately at Perth Amboy and at Burlington. Lord Cornbury, the first governor, was also Governor of

New York, a humiliating arrangement that led to no end of trouble. The executive government, the press, and the judiciary were in the complete control of the Crown and the Governor, who was instructed to take care that "God Almighty be duly served according to the rites of the Church of England, and the traffic in merchantable negroes encouraged." Cornbury contemptuously ignored the assembly's right to adjourn and kept adjourning it till one was elected which would pass the laws he wanted. Afterwards the assemblies were less compliant, and, under the lead of two able men, Lewis Morris of East Jersey and Samuel Jennings, a Quaker of West Jersey, they stood up for their rights and complained to the mother country. But Cornbury went on fighting them, granted monopolies, established arbitrary fees, prohibited the proprietors from selling their lands, prevented three members of the assembly duly elected from being sworn, and was absent in New York so much of the time that the laws went unexecuted and convicted murderers wandered about at large. In short, he went through pretty much the whole list of offenses of a corrupt and good-for-nothing royal governor of colonial times. The union of the two colonies consequently seemed to involve no improvement over former conditions. At last, the protests and appeals of proprietors and people prevailed, and Cornbury was recalled.

Quieter times followed, and in 1738 New Jersey had the satisfaction of obtaining a governor all her own. The New York Governor had always neglected Jersey affairs, was difficult of access, made appointments and administered justice in the interests of New York, and forced Jersey vessels to pay registration fees to New York. Amid great rejoicing over the change, the Crown appointed the popular leader, Lewis Morris, as governor. But by a strange turn of fate, when once secure in power, he became a most obstinate upholder of royal prerogative, worried the assembly with adjournments, and, after Cornbury, was the most obnoxious of all the royal governors.

The governors now usually made Burlington their capital and it became, on that account, a place of much show and interest. The last colonial governor was William Franklin, an illegitimate son of Benjamin Franklin, and he would probably have made a success of the office if the Revolution had not stopped him. He had plenty of ability, affable manners, and was full of humor and anecdote like his father, whom he is said to have

somewhat resembled.   He had combined in youth a
fondness for books with a fondness for adventure,
was comptroller of the colonial post office and clerk
of the Pennsylvania Assembly, served a couple
of campaigns in the French and Indian Wars, went
to England with his father in 1757, was admitted to
the English Bar, attained some intimacy with the
Earl of Bute and Lord Fairfax, and through the latter obtained the governorship of New Jersey in 1762.

The people were at first much displeased at his appointment and never entirely got over his illegitimate birth and his turning from Whig to Tory as
soon as his appointment was secured.   But he advanced the interests of the colony with the home
government and favored beneficial legislation.   He
had an attractive wife, and they entertained, it is
said, with viceregal elegance, and started a fine
model farm or country place on the north shore of
the Rancocas not far from the capital at Burlington.
Franklin was drawing the province together and
building it up as a community, but his extreme loyalist principles in the Revolution destroyed his chance
for popularity and have obscured his reputation.

Though the population of New Jersey was a
mixed one, judged by the very distinct religious

differences of colonial times, yet racially it was thoroughly Anglo-Saxon and a good stock to build upon. At the time of the Revolution in 1776 the people numbered only about 120,000, indicating a slow growth; but when the first census of the United States was taken, in 1790, they numbered 184,139.

The natural division of the State into North and South Jersey is marked by a line from Trenton to Jersey City. The people of these two divisions were quite as distinct in early times as striking differences in environment and religion could make them. Even in the inevitable merging of modern life the two regions are still distinct socially, economically, and intellectually. Along the dividing line the two types of the population, of course, merged and here was produced and is still to be found the Jerseyman of the composite type.

Trenton, the capital of the State, is very properly in the dividing belt. It was named after William Trent, a Philadelphia merchant who had been speaker of the Pennsylvania Assembly and who became chief justice of New Jersey. Long ages before white men came Trenton seems to have been a meeting place and residence of the Indians or preceding races of stone age men. Antiquarians have estimated that fifty thousand stone implements have been found in it. As it was at the head of tidewater, at the so-called Falls of the Delaware, it was apparently a center of travel and traffic from other regions. From the top of the bluff below the modern city of Trenton there was easy access to forests of chestnut, oak, and pine, with their supplies of game, while the river and its tributary creeks were full of fish. It was a pleasant and convenient place where the people of prehistoric times apparently met and lingered during many centuries without necessarily having a large resident population at any one time. Trenton was so obviously convenient and central in colonial times that it was seriously proposed as a site for the national capital.

Princeton University, though originating, as we have seen, among the Presbyterians of North Jersey, seems as a higher educational institution for the whole State to belong naturally in the dividing belt, the meeting place of the two divisions of the colony. The college began its existence at Elizabeth, was then moved to Newark, both in the strongly Presbyterian region, and finally, in 1757, was established at Princeton, a more suitable place, it was thought, because far removed from the dissipation and temptation of towns, and because it was in the center of the colony on the post road between Philadelphia and New York. Though chartered as the College of New Jersey, it was often called Nassau Hall at Princeton or simply "Princeton." In 1896 it became known officially as Princeton University. It was a hard struggle to found the college with lotteries and petty subscriptions here and there. But Presbyterians in New York and other provinces gave aid. Substantial assistance was also obtained from the Presbyterians of England and Scotland. In the old pamphlets of the time which have been preserved the founders of the college argued that higher education was needed not only for ministers of religion, but for the bench, the bar, and the legislature. The two New England colleges, Harvard and Yale, on the north, and the Virginia College of William and Mary on the south, were too far away. There must be a college close at hand.

At first most of the graduates entered the Presbyterian ministry. But soon in the short time before the Revolution there were produced statesmen such as Richard Stockton of New Jersey, who signed the Declaration of Independence; physicians such as Dr. Benjamin Rush of Philadelphia; soldiers such as "Light Horse" Harry Lee of Virginia; as well as founders of other colleges, governors of States, lawyers, attorney-generals, judges, congressmen, and indeed a very powerful assemblage of intellectual lights. Nor should the names of James Madison, Aaron Burr, and Jonathan Edwards be omitted.

East Jersey with her New England influence attempted something like free public schools. In West Jersey the Quakers had schools. In both Jerseys, after 1700 some private neighborhood schools were started, independent of religious denominations. The West Jersey Quakers, self-cultured and with a very effective system of mental discipline and education in their families as well as in their schools, were not particularly interested in higher education. But in East Jersey as another evidence of intellectual awakening in colonial times, Queen's College, afterward known as Rutgers College, was established by the Dutch Reformed Church in 1766, and was naturally placed, near the old source of Dutch influence, at New Brunswick in the northerly end of the dividing belt.

New Jersey was fortunate in having no Indian

wars in colonial times, no frontier, no point of
hostile contact with the French of Canada or with
the powerful western tribes of red men. Like
Rhode Island in this respect, she was completely
shut in by the other colonies. Once or twice only did
bands of savages cross the Delaware and commit
depredations on Jersey soil. This colony, however,
did her part in sending troops and assistance to the
others in the long French and Indian wars; but she
had none of the pressing danger and experience of
other colonies. Her people were never drawn together by a common danger until the Revolution.

In Jersey colonial homes there was not a single
modern convenience of light, heat, or cooking, and
none of the modern amusements. But there was
plenty of good living and simple diversion — husk-
ing bees and shooting in the autumn, skating and
sleighing in the winter. Meetings and discussions
in coffeehouses and inns supplied in those days the
place of our modern books, newspapers, and maga-
zines. Jersey inns were famous meeting places.
Everybody passed through their doors — judges,
lawyers, legislators, politicians, post riders, stage
drivers, each bringing his contribution of information and humor, and the slaves and rabble stood
round to pick up news and see the fun.

The court days in each county were holidays celebrated with games of quoits, running, jumping, feasting, and discussions political and social. At the capital there was even style and extravagance. Governor Belcher, for example, who lived at Burlington, professed to believe that the Quaker influences of that town were not strict enough in keeping the Sabbath, so he drove every Sunday in his coach and four to Philadelphia to worship in the Presbyterian Church there and saw no inconsistency in his own behavior.

Almanacs furnished much of the reading for the masses. The few newspapers offered little except the barest chronicle of events. The books of the upper classes were good though few, and consisted chiefly of the classics of English literature and books of information and travel. The diaries and letters of colonial native Jerseymen, the pamphlets of the time, and John Woolman's *Journal*, all show a good average of education and an excellent use of the English language. Samuel Smith's *History of the Colony of Nova-Cæsaria, or New Jersey*, written and printed at Burlington and published there in the year 1765, is written in a good and even attractive style, with as intelligent a grasp of political events as any modern mind could show; the type, paper, and presswork, too, are excellent. Smith was born and educated in this same New Jersey town. He became a member of council and assembly, at one time was treasurer of the province, and his manuscript historical collections were largely used by Robert Proud in his *History of Pennsylvania.*

The early houses of New Jersey were of heavy timbers covered with unpainted clapboards, usually one story and a half high, with immense fireplaces, which, with candles, supplied the light. The floors were scrubbed hard and sprinkled with the plentiful white sand. Carpets, except the famous old rag carpets, were very rare. The old wooden houses have now almost entirely disappeared; but many of the brick houses which succeeded them are still preserved. They are of simple well-proportioned architecture, of a distinctive type, less luxuriant, massive, and exuberant than those across the river in Pennsylvania, although both evidently derived from the Christopher Wren school. The old Jersey homes seem to reflect with great exactness the simple feeling of the people and to be one expression of the spirit of Jersey democracy.

There were no important seats of commerce in

this province. Exports of wheat, provisions, and lumber went to Philadelphia or New York, which were near and convenient. The Jersey shores near the mouth of the Hudson and along the Delaware, as at Camden, presented opportunities for ports, but the proximity to the two dominating ports prevented the development of additional harbors in this part of the coast. It was not until after the Revolution that Camden, opposite Philadelphia, and Jersey City, opposite New York, grew into anything like their present importance.

There were, however, a number of small ports and shipbuilding villages in the Jerseys. It is a noticeable fact that in colonial times and even later there were very few Jersey towns beyond the head of tidewater. The people, even the farmers, were essentially maritime. The province showed its natural maritime characteristics, produced many sailors, and built innumerable small vessels for the coasting and West India trade — sloops, schooners, yachts, and sailboats, down to the tiniest gunning boat and sneak box. Perth Amboy was the principal port and shipbuilding center for East Jersey as Salem was for West Jersey. But Burlington, Bordentown, Cape May, and Trenton, and innumerable little villages up creeks and channels or mere ditches could not be kept from the prevailing industry. They built craft up to the limit of size that could be floated away in the water before their very doors. Plentifully supplied with excellent oak and pine and with the admirable white cedar of their own forests, very skillful shipwrights grew up in every little hamlet.

A large part of the capital used in Jersey ship-building is said to have come from Philadelphia and New York. At first this capital sought its profit in whaling along the coast and afterwards in the trade with the West Indies, which for a time absorbed so much of the shipping of all the colonies in America. The inlets and beaches along the Jersey coast now given over to summer resorts were first used for whaling camps or bases. Cape May and Tuckerton were started and maintained by whaling; and as late as 1830, it is said, there were still signs of the industry on Long Beach.

Except for the whaling, the beaches were uninhabited — wild stretches of sand, swarming with birds and wild fowl, without a lighthouse or life-saving station. In the Revolution, when the British fleet blockaded the Delaware and New York, Little Egg, the safest of the inlets, was used for evading the blockade. Vessels entered there and sailed up the Mullica River to the head of navigation, whence the goods were distributed by wagons. To conceal their vessels when anchored just inside an inlet, the privateersmen would stand slim pine trees beside the masts and thus very effectively concealed the rigging from British cruisers prowling along the shore.

Along with the whaling industry the risks and seclusion of the inlets and channels developed a romantic class of gentlemen, as handy with musket and cutlass as with helm and sheet, fond of easy, exciting profits, and reaping where they had not sown. They would start legally enough, for they began as privateersmen under legal letters of marque in the wars. But the step was a short one to a traffic still more profitable; and for a hundred years Jersey customs officers are said to have issued documents which were ostensibly letters of marque but which really abetted a piratical cruise. Piracy was, however, in those days a semilegitimate offense, winked at by the authorities all through the colonial period; and respectable people and governors and officials of New York and North Carolina, it is said, secretly furnished funds for such expeditions and were interested in the profits.

CHAPTER XII

LITTLE DELAWARE

DELAWARE was the first colony to be established on the river that bears this name. It went through half a century of experiences under the Dutch and Swedes from 1609 to 1664, and then eighteen years under the English rule of the Duke of York, from whom it passed into the hands of William Penn, the Quaker. The Dutch got into it by an accident and were regarded by the English as interlopers. And the Swedes who followed had no better title.

The whole North Atlantic seaboard was claimed by England by virtue of the discoveries of the Cabots, father and son; but more than a hundred years elapsed before England took advantage of this claim by starting the Virginia colony near the mouth of the Chesapeake Bay in 1607. And nearly a quarter of a century more elapsed before Englishmen settled on the shores of Massachusetts

Bay. Those were the two points most accessible to ships and most favorable for settlement. The middle ground of the Delaware and Hudson regions was not so easily entered and remained unoccupied. The mouth of the Delaware was full of shoals and was always difficult to navigate. The natural harbor at the mouth of the Hudson was excellent, but the entrance to it was not at first apparent.

Into these two regions, however, the Dutch chanced just after the English had effected the settlement of Jamestown in Virginia. The Dutch had employed an Englishman named Henry Hudson and sent him in 1609 in a small ship called the *Half Moon* to find a passage to China and India by way of the Arctic Ocean. Turned back by the ice in the Arctic, he sailed down the coast of North America and began exploring the middle ground from the Virginia settlement, which he seems to have known about; and, working cautiously northward along the coast and feeling his way with the lead line, he soon entered Delaware Bay. But finding it very difficult of navigation he departed and, proceeding in the same careful way up along the coast of New Jersey, he finally entered the harbor of New York and sailed up the Hudson far enough to satisfy himself that it was not the desired course to China.

This exploration gave the Dutch their claim to the Delaware and Hudson regions. But though it was worthless as against the English right by discovery of the Cabots, the Dutch went ahead with their settlement, established their headquarters and seat of government on Manhattan Island, where New York stands today, and exercised as much jurisdiction and control as they could on the Delaware.

Their explorations of the Delaware, feeling their way up it with small light draft vessels among its shoals and swift tides, their travels on land — shooting wild turkeys on the site of the present busy town of Chester — and their adventures with the Indians are full of interest. The immense quantities of wild fowl and animal and bird life along the shores astonished them; but what most aroused their cupidity was the enormous supply of furs, especially beaver and otter, that could be obtained from the Indians. Furs became their great, in fact, their only interest in the Delaware. They established forts, one near Cape Henlopen at the mouth of the river, calling it Fort Oplandt, and another far up the river on the Jersey side at the mouth of Timber Creek, nearly opposite the present site of Philadelphia, and this they called Fort Nassau. Fort Oplandt was destroyed by the Indians and its people were massacred. Fort Nassau was probably occupied only at intervals. These two posts were built mainly to assist the fur trade, and any attempts at real settlement were slight and unsuccessful.

Meantime about the year 1624 the Swedes heard of the wonderful opportunities on the Delaware. The Swedish monarch, Gustavus Adolphus, a man of broad ambitions and energetic mind, heard about the Delaware from Willem Usselinx, a merchant of Antwerp who had been actively interested in the formation of the Dutch West India Company to trade in the Dutch possessions in America. Having quarreled with the directors, Usselinx had withdrawn from the Netherlands and now offered his services to Sweden. The Swedish court, nobles, and people, all became enthusiastic about the project which he elaborated for a great commercial company to trade and colonize in Asia, Africa, and America.[1] But the plan was dropped because, soon after 1630, Gustavus Adolphus led his country

[1] See *Willem Usselinx*, by J. F. Jameson in the *Papers of the American Historical Association*, vol. II.

to intervene on the side of the Protestants in the Thirty Years' War in Germany, where he was killed three years later at the battle of Lützen. But the desire aroused by Usselinx for a Swedish colonial empire was revived in the reign of his infant daughter, Christina, by the celebrated Swedish Chancellor, Oxenstierna.

An expedition, which actually reached the Delaware in 1638, was sent out under another Dutch renegade, Peter Minuit, who had been Governor of New Netherland and after being dismissed from office was now leading this Swedish enterprise to occupy part of the territory he had formerly governed for the Dutch. His two ships sailed up the Delaware and with good judgment landed at the present site of Wilmington. At that point a creek carrying a depth of over fourteen feet for ten miles from its mouth flowed into the Delaware. The Dutch had called this creek Minquas, after the tribe of Indians; the Swedes named it the Christina after their infant Queen; and in modern times it has been corrupted into Christiana.

They sailed about two and a half miles through its delta marshes to some rocks which formed a natural wharf and which still stand today at the foot of Sixth Street in Wilmington. This was the

Plymouth Rock of Delaware. Level land, marshes, and meadows lay along the Christina, the remains of the delta which the stream had formed in the past. On the edge of the delta or moorland, rocky hills rose, forming the edge of the Piedmont, and out of them from the north flowed a fine large stream, the Brandywine, which fell into the Christina just before it entered the Delaware. Here in the delta their engineer laid out a town, called Christinaham, and a fort behind the rocks on which they had landed. A cove in the Christina made a snug anchorage for their ships, out of the way of the tide. They then bought from the Indians all the land from Cape Henlopen to the Falls of the Delaware at Trenton, calling it New Sweden and the Delaware New Swedeland Stream. The people of Delaware have always regarded New Sweden as the beginning of their State, and Peter Minuit, the leader of this Swedish expedition, always stands first on the published lists of their governors.

On their arrival in the river in the spring of 1638, the Swedes found no evidences of permanent Dutch colonization. Neither Fort Oplandt nor Fort Nassau was then occupied. They always maintained that the Dutch had abandoned the river, and that it was therefore open to the Swedes for occupation, especially after they had purchased the Indian title. It was certainly true that the Dutch efforts to plant colonies in that region had failed; and since the last attempt by De Vries, six years had elapsed. On the other hand, the Dutch contended that they had in that time put Fort Nassau in repair, although they had not occupied it, and that they kept a few persons living along the Jersey shore of the river, possibly the remains of the Nassau colony, to watch all who visited it. These people had immediately notified the Dutch governor Kieft at New Amsterdam of the arrival of the Swedes, and he promptly issued a protest against the intrusion. But his protest was neither very strenuous nor was it followed up by hostile action, for Sweden and Holland were on friendly terms. Sweden, the great champion of Protestant Europe, had intervened in the Thirty Years' War to save the Protestants of Germany. The Dutch had just finished a similar desperate war of eighty years for freedom from the papal despotism of Spain. Dutch and Swedes had, therefore, every reason to be in sympathy with each other.

The Swedes, a plain, strong, industrious people,

as William Penn aptly called them, were soon, however, seriously interfering with the Dutch fur trade and in the first year, it is said, collected thirty thousand skins. If this is true, it is an indication of the immense supply of fur-bearing animals, especially beaver, available at that time. For the next twenty-five years Dutch and Swedes quarreled and sometimes fought over their respective claims. But it is significant of the difficulty of retaining a hold on the Delaware region that the Swedish colonists on the Christina after a year or two regarded themselves as a failure and were on the point of abandoning their enterprise, when a vessel fortunately for them arrived with cattle, agricultural tools, and immigrants. It is significant also that the immigrants, though in a Swedish vessel and under the Swedish government, were Dutchmen. They formed a sort of separate Dutch colony under Swedish rule and settled near St. George's and Appoquinimink. Immigrants apparently were difficult to obtain among the Swedes, who were not colonizers like the English.

At this very time, in fact, Englishmen, Puritans from Connecticut, were slipping into the Delaware region under the leadership of Nathaniel Turner and George Lamberton, and were buying the land from the Indians. About sixty settled near Salem, New Jersey, and some on the Schuylkill in Pennsylvania, close to Fort Nassau — an outrageous piece of audacity, said the Dutch, and an insult to their "High Mightinesses and the noble Directors of the West India Company." So the Schuylkill English were accordingly driven out, and their houses were burned. The Swedes afterwards expelled the English from Salem and from the Cohansey, lower down the Bay. Later the English were allowed to return, but they seem to have done little except trade for furs and beat off hostile Indians.

The seat of the Swedish government was moved in 1643 from the Christina to Tinicum, one of the islands of the Schuylkill delta, with an excellent harbor in front of it which is now the home of the yacht clubs of Philadelphia. Here they built a fort of logs, called Fort Gothenborg, a chapel with a graveyard, and a mansion house for the governor, and this remained the seat of Swedish authority as long as they had any on the river. From here Governor Printz, a portly irascible old soldier, said to have weighed "upwards of 400 pounds and taken three drinks at every meal," ruled the river. He built forts on the Schuylkill and worried the Dutch out of the fur trade. He also built a fort called Nya Elfsborg, afterward Elsinboro, on the Jersey side below Salem. By means of this fort he was able to command the entrance to the river and compelled every Dutch ship to strike her colors and acknowledge the sovereignty of Sweden. Some he prevented from going up the river at all; others he allowed to pass on payment of toll or tribute. He gave orders to destroy every trading house or fort which the Dutch had built on the Schuylkill, and to tear down the coat of arms and insignia which the Dutch had placed on a post on the site of Philadelphia. The Swedes now also bought from the Indians and claimed the land on the Jersey side from Cape May up to Raccoon Creek, opposite the modern Chester.

The best place to trade with the Indians for furs was the Schuylkill River, which flowed into the Delaware at a point where Philadelphia was afterwards built. There were at that time Indian villages where West Philadelphia now stands. The headwaters of streams flowing into the Schuylkill were only a short distance from the headwaters of streams flowing into the Susquehanna, so that the valley of the Schuylkill formed the natural highway into the interior of Pennsylvania. The route to the Ohio River followed the Schuylkill for some thirty or forty miles, turned up one of its tributaries to its source, then crossed the watershed to the head of a stream flowing into the Susquehanna, thence to the Juniata, at the head of which the trail led over a short divide to the head of the Conemaugh, which flowed into the Allegheny, and the Allegheny into the Ohio. Some of the Swedes and Dutch appear to have followed this route with the Indians as early as 1646.

The Ohio and Allegheny region was inhabited by the Black Minquas, so called from their custom of wearing a black badge on their breast. The Ohio, indeed, was first called the Black Minquas River. As the country nearer the Delaware was gradually denuded of beaver, these Black Minquas became the great source of supply and carried the furs, over the route described, to the Schuylkill. The White Minquas lived further east, round Chesapeake and Delaware bays, and, though spoken of as belonging by language to the great Iroquois or Six Nation stock, were themselves conquered and pretty much exterminated by the Six Nations. The Black Minquas, believed to be the same as the Eries of the Jesuit Relations, were also practically exterminated by the Six Nations.[1]

[1] Myers, *Narratives of Early Pennsylvania*, pp. 103–104.

The furs brought down the Schuylkill were deposited at certain rocks two or three miles above its mouth at Bartram's Gardens, now one of the city parks of Philadelphia. On these rocks, then an island in the Schuylkill, the Swedes built a fort which completely commanded the river and cut the Dutch off from the fur trade. They built another fort on the other side of Bartram's Gardens along the meadow near what is now Gibson's Point; and Governor Printz had a great mill a couple of miles away on Cobb's Creek, where the old Blue Bell tavern has long stood. These two forts protected the mill and the Indian villages in West Philadelphia.

One would like to revisit the Delaware of those days and see all its wild life and game, its islands and shoals, its virgin forests as they had grown up since the glacial age, untouched by the civilization of the white man. There were then more islands in the river, the water was clearer, and there were pretty pebble and sandy beaches now overlaid by mud brought down from vast regions of the valley no longer protected by forests from the wash of the rains. On a wooded island below Salem, long since cut away by the tides, the pirate Blackbeard and his crew are said to have passed a winter. The waters of the river spread out wide at every high tide over marshes and meadows, turning them twice a day for a few hours into lakes, grown up in summer with red and yellow flowers and the graceful wild oats, or reeds, tasseled like Indian corn.

At Christinaham, in the delta of the Christina and the Brandywine, the tide flowed far inland to the rocks on which Minuit's Swedish expedition landed, leaving one dry spot called Cherry Island, a name still borne by a shoal in the river. Fort Christina, on the edge of the overflowed meadow, with the rocky promontory of hills behind it, its church and houses, and a wide prospect across the delta and river, was a fair spot in the old days. The Indians came down the Christina in their canoes or overland, bringing their packs of beaver, otter, and deer skins, their tobacco, corn, and venison to exchange for the cloth, blankets, tools, and gaudy trinkets that pleased them. It must often have been a scene of strange life and coloring, and it is difficult today to imagine it all occurring close to the spot where the Pennsylvania railroad station now stands in Wilmington.

When doughty Peter Stuyvesant became Governor of New Netherland, he determined to assert Dutch authority once more on the South River, as the Delaware was called in distinction from the

14

Hudson. As the Swedes now controlled it by their three forts, not a Dutch ship could reach Fort Nassau without being held up at Fort Elfsborg or at Fort Christina or at the fort at Tinicum. It was a humiliating situation for the haughty spirit of the Dutch governor. To open the river to Dutch commerce again, Stuyvesant marched overland in 1651 through the wilderness, with one hundred and twenty men and, abandoning Fort Nassau, built a new fort on a fine promontory which then extended far out into the river below Christina. Today the place is known as New Castle; the Dutch commonly referred to it as Sandhoeck or Sand Point; the English called it Grape Vine Point. Stuyvesant named it Fort Casimir.

The tables were now turned: the Dutch could retaliate upon Swedish shipping. But the Swedes were not so easily to be dispossessed. Three years later a new Swedish governor named Rising arrived in the river with a number of immigrants and soldiers. He sailed straight up to Fort Casimir, took it by surprise, and ejected the Dutch garrison of about a dozen men. As the successful coup occurred on Trinity Sunday, the Swedes renamed the place Fort Trinity.

The whole population — Dutch and Swede, but

in 1654 mostly Swede — numbered only 368 persons. Before the arrival of Rising there had been only seventy. It seems a very small number about which to be writing history; but small as it was their "High Mightinesses," as the government of the United Netherlands was called, were determined to avenge on even so small a number the insult of the capture of Fort Casimir.

Drums, it is said, were beaten every day in Holland to call for recruits to go to America. Gunners, carpenters, and powder were collected. A ship of war was sent from Holland, accompanied by two other vessels whose names alone, *Great Christopher* and *King Solomon*, should have been sufficient to scare all the Swedes. At New Amsterdam, Stuyvesant labored night and day to fit out the expedition. A French privateer which happened to be in the harbor was hired. Several other vessels, in all seven ships, and six or seven hundred men, with a chaplain called Megapolensis, composed this mighty armament gathered together to drive out the handful of poor hardworking Swedes. A day of fasting and prayer was held and the Almighty was implored to bless this mighty expedition which, He was assured, was undertaken for "the glory of His name."

It was the absurdity of such contrasts as this running all through the annals of the Dutch in America that inspired Washington Irving to write his infinitely humorous *History of New York from the Beginning of the World to the End of the Dutch Dynasty*, by "Diedrich Knickerbocker." It is difficult for an Anglo-Saxon to take the Dutch in America seriously. What can you do with a people whose imagination allowed them to give such names to their ships as *Weigh Scales*, *Spotted Cow*, and *The Pear Tree?* So Irving described the taking of Fort Casimir in mock heroic manner. He describes the marshaling of the Dutch hosts of New York by families, the Van Grolls of Anthony's Nose, the Brinkerhoffs, the Van Kortlandts, the Van Bunschotens of Nyack and Kakiat, the fighting men of Wallabout, the Van Pelts, the Suy Dams, the Van Dams, and all the warriors of Hellgate "clad in their thunder-and-lightning gaberdines," and lastly the standard bearers and bodyguards of Peter Stuyvesant, bearing the great beaver of the Manhattan.

And now commenced the horrid din, the desperate struggle, the maddening ferocity, the frantic desperation, the confusion and self-abandonment of war. Dutchman and Swede commingled, tugged, panted, and blowed. The heavens were darkened with a tempest of missives. Bang! went the guns; whack! went the broadswords; thump! went the cudgels; crash! went the musket-stocks; blows, kicks, cuffs, scratches, black eyes and bloody noses swelling the horrors of the scene! Thick, thwack, cut and hack, helter-skelter, higgledy-piggledy, hurly-burly, heads-over-heels, rough-and-tumble! Dunder and blixum! swore the Dutchmen; splitter and splutter! cried the Swedes. Storm the works! shouted Hardkoppig Peter. Fire the mine! roared stout Risingh— Tantarar-ra-ra! twanged the trumpet of Antony Van Corlear; — until all voice and sound became unintelligible, — grunts of pain, yells of fury, and shouts of triumph mingling in one hideous clamor. The earth shook as if struck with a paralytic stroke; trees shrunk aghast, and withered at the sight; rocks burrowed in the ground like rabbits; and even Christina creek turned from its course, and ran up a hill in breathless terror!

As a matter of fact, the fort surrendered without a fight on September 1, 1655. It was thereupon christened New Amstel, afterwards New Castle, and was for a long time the most important town on the Delaware. This achievement put the Dutch in complete authority over the Swedes on both sides of the river. The Swedes, however, were content, abandoned politics, secluded themselves on their farms, and left politics to the Dutch. Trade, too, they left to the Dutch, who, in their effort to monopolize it, almost killed it.

This conquest by their High Mightinesses also ended the attempts of the New Englanders, particularly the people of New Haven, to get a foothold in the neighborhood of Salem, New Jersey, for which they had been struggling for years. They had dreams of a great lake far to northward full of beaver to which the Delaware would lead them. Their efforts to establish themselves survived in one or two names of places near Salem, as, for example, New England Creek, and New England Channel, which down almost into our own time was found on charts marking one of the minor channels of the bay along the Jersey shore. They continued coming to the river in ships to trade in spite of restrictions by the Dutch; and some of them in later years, as has been pointed out, secured a foothold on the Cohansey and in the Cape May region, where their descendants are still to be found.

CHAPTER XIII

THE ENGLISH CONQUEST

It is a curious fact that the ancestor of the numerous Beekman family in New York, after whom Beekman Street is named, was for a time one of the Dutch governors on the Delaware who afterwards became the sheriff of Esopus, New York. His successor on the Delaware had some thoughts of removing the capital down to Odessa on the Appoquinimink, when an event long dreaded happened. In 1664, war broke out between England and Holland, long rivals in trade and commerce, and all the Dutch possessions in the New World fell an easy prey to English conquerors. A British fleet took possession of New Amsterdam, which surrendered without a struggle. But when two British men of war under Sir Robert Carr appeared before New Amstel on the Delaware, Governor D'Hinoyossa unwisely resisted; and his untenable fort was quickly subdued by a few broadsides and a storming party. This opposition gave the conquering party, according to the custom of the times, the right to plunder; and it must be confessed that the English soldiers made full use of their opportunity. They plundered the town and confiscated the land of prominent citizens for the benefit of the officers of the expedition.

After the English conquest on the Delaware, not a few of the Dutch migrated to Maryland, where their descendants, it is said, are still to be found. Some in later years returned to the Delaware, where on the whole, notwithstanding the early confiscations, English rule seemed to promise well. The very first documents, the terms of surrender both on the Delaware and on the Hudson, breathed an air of Anglo-Saxon freedom. Everybody was at liberty to come and go at will. Hollanders could migrate to the Delaware or to New York as much as before. The Dutch soldiers in the country, if they wished to remain, were to have fifty acres of land apiece. This generous settlement seemed in striking contrast to the pinching, narrow interference with trade and individual rights, the seizures and confiscations for private gain, all under pretense of punishment, bad enough on the Delaware but worse at New Amsterdam, which had characterized the rule of the Dutch.

The Duke of York, to whom Delaware was given, introduced trial by jury, settled private titles, and left undisturbed the religion and local customs of the people. But the political rule of the Duke was absolute as became a Stuart. He arbitrarily taxed exports and imports. Executive, judicial, and legislative powers were all vested in his deputy governor at New York or in creatures appointed and controlled by him. It was the sort of government the Duke hoped to impose upon all Great Britain when he should come to the throne, and he was trying his 'prentice hand in the colonies. A political rebellion against this despotism was started on the Delaware by a man named Konigsmarke, or the Long Finn, aided by an Englishman, Henry Coleman. They were captured and tried for treason, their property was confiscated, and the Long Finn branded with the letter R, and sold as a slave in the Barbados. They might be called the first martyrs to foreshadow the English Revolution of 1688 which ended forever the despotic reign of the Stuarts.

The Swedes continued to form the main body of people on the Delaware under the régime of the Duke of York, and at the time when William Penn took possession of the country in 1682 their settlements extended from New Castle up through Christina, Marcus Hook, Upland (now Chester), Tinicum, Kingsessing in the modern West Philadelphia, Passyunk, Wicaco, both in modern Philadelphia, and as far up the river as Frankford and Pennypack. They had their churches at Christina, Tinicum, Kingsessing, and Wicaco. The last, when absorbed by Philadelphia, was a pretty little hamlet on the river shore, its farms belonging to a Swedish family called Swanson whose name is now borne by one of the city's streets. Across the river in New Jersey, opposite Chester, the Swedes had settlements on Raccoon Creek and round Swedesboro. These river settlements constituted an interesting and from all accounts a very attractive Scandinavian community. Their strongest bond of union seems to have been their interest in their Lutheran churches on the river. They spread very little into the interior, made few roads, and lived almost exclusively on the river or on its navigable tributaries. One reason they gave for this preference was that it was easier to reach the different churches by boat.

There were only about a thousand Swedes along the Delaware and possibly five hundred of Dutch and mixed blood, together with a few English, all living a life of abundance on a fine river amid pleasing scenery, with good supplies of fish and game, a fertile soil, and a wilderness of opportunity to the west of them. All were well pleased to be relieved from the stagnant despotism of the Duke of York and to take part in the free popular government of William Penn in Pennsylvania. They became magistrates and officials, members of the council and of the legislature. They soon found that all their avenues of trade and life were quickened. They passed from mere farmers supplying their own needs to exporters of the products of their farms.

Descendants of the Swedes and Dutch still form the basis of the population of Delaware.[1] There were some Finns at Marcus Hook, which was called Finland; and it may be noted in passing that there were not a few French among the Dutch, as among the Germans in Pennsylvania,

---

[1] Swedish names anglicized are now found everywhere. Gostafsson has become Justison and Justis. Bond has become Boon; Hoppman, Hoffman; Kalsberg, Colesberry; Wihler, Wheeler; Joccom, Yocum; Dahlbo, Dalbow; Konigh, King; Kyn, Keen; and so on. Then there are also such names as Wallraven, Hendrickson, Stedham, Peterson, Matson, Talley, Anderson, and the omnipresent Rambo, which have suffered little, if any, change. Dutch names are also numerous, such as Lockermans, Vandever, Van Dyke, Vangezel, Vandegrift, Alricks, Statts, Van Zandt, Hyatt, Cochran (originally Kolchman), Vance, and Blackstone (originally Blackenstein).

Huguenots who had fled from religious persecution in France. The name Jaquette, well known in Delaware, marks one of these families, whose immigrant ancestor was one of the Dutch governors. In the ten or dozen generations since the English conquest intermarriage has in many instances inextricably mixed up Swede, Dutch, and French, as well as the English stock, so that many persons with Dutch names are of Swedish or French descent and vice versa, and some with English names like Oldham are of Dutch descent. There has been apparently much more intermarriage among the different nationalities in the province and less standing aloof than among the alien divisions of Pennsylvania.

After the English conquest some Irish Presbyterians or Scotch-Irish entered Delaware. Finally came the Quakers, comparatively few in colonial times but more numerous after the Revolution, especially in Wilmington and its neighborhood. True to their characteristics, they left descendants who have become the most prominent and useful citizens down into our own time. At present Wilmington has become almost as distinctive a Quaker town as Philadelphia. "Thee" and "thou" are frequently heard in the streets, and a surprisingly large proportion of the people of prominence and importance are Quakers or of Quaker descent. Many of the neat and pleasant characteristics of the town are distinctly of Quaker origin; and these characteristics are found wherever Quaker influence prevails.

Wilmington was founded about 1731 by Thomas Willing, an Englishman, who had married into the Swedish family of Justison. He laid out a few streets on his wife's land on the hill behind the site of old Fort Christina, in close imitation of the plan of Philadelphia, and from that small beginning the present city grew, and was at first called Willingtown.[1] William Shipley, a Pennsylvania Quaker born in England, bought land in it in 1735, and having more capital than Willing, pushed the fortunes of the town more rapidly. He probably had not a little to do with bringing Quakers to Wilmington; indeed, their first meetings were held in a house belonging to him until they could build a meeting house of their own in 1738.

Both Shipley and Willing had been impressed with the natural beauty of the situation, the wide view over the level moorland and green marsh

[1] Some years later in a borough charter granted by Penn, the name was changed to Wilmington in honor of the Earl of Wilmington.

and across the broad river to the Jersey shore, as well as by the natural conveniences of the place for trade and commerce. Wilmington has ever since profited by its excellent situation, with the level moorland for industry, the river for traffic, and the first terraces or hills of the Piedmont for residence; and, for scenery, the Brandywine tumbling through rocks and bowlders in a long series of rapids.

The custom still surviving in Wilmington of punishing certain classes of criminals by whipping appears to have originated in the days of Willing and Shipley, about the year 1740, when a cage, stocks, and whipping-post were erected. They were placed in the most conspicuous part of the town, and there the culprit, in addition to his legal punishment, was also disciplined at the discretion of passers-by with rotten eggs and other equally potent encouragements to reform. These gratuitous inflictions, not mentioned in the statute, as well as the public exhibition of the prisoner were abolished in later times and in this modified form the method of correction was extended to the two other counties. Sometimes a cat-o'-nine-tails was used, sometimes a rawhide whip, and sometimes a switch cut from a tree. Nowadays, however, all the whipping for the State is done in Wilmington, where all prisoners sentenced to whipping in the State are sent. This punishment is found to be so efficacious that its infliction a second time on the same person is exceedingly rare.

The most striking relic of the old Swedish days in Wilmington is the brick and stone church of good proportions and no small beauty, and today one of the very ancient relics of America. It was built by the Swedes in 1698 to replace their old wooden church, which was on the lower land, and the Swedish language was used in the services down to the year 1800, when the building was turned over to the Church of England. Old Peter Minuit, the first Swedish governor, may possibly have been buried there. The Swedes built another pretty chapel — Gloria Dei, as it was called — at the village of Wicaco, on the shore of the Delaware where Philadelphia afterwards was established. The original building was taken down in 1700, and the present one was erected on its site partly with materials from the church at Tinicum. It remained Swedish Lutheran until 1831, when, like all the Swedish chapels, it became the property of the Church of England, between which and the Swedish Lutheran body there was a close affinity, if not in doctrine, at least in episcopal organization.[1] The old brick church dating from 1740, on the main street of Wilmington, is an interesting relic of the colonial Scotch-Irish Presbyterians in Delaware, and is now carefully preserved as the home of the Historical Society.

After Delaware had been eighteen years under the Duke of York, William Penn felt a need of the west side of the river all the way down to the sea to strengthen his ownership of Pennsylvania. He also wanted to offset the ambitions of Lord Baltimore to extend Maryland northward. Penn accordingly persuaded his friend James, the Duke of York, to give him a grant of Delaware, which Penn thereupon annexed to Pennsylvania under the name of the Territories or Three Lower Counties. The three counties, New Castle, Kent, and Sussex,[2] are still the counties of Delaware, each one extending across the State and filling its whole length from the hills of the Brandywine on the Pennsylvania border to the sands of Sussex at Cape Henlopen. The term "Territory" has ever since been used in America to describe an outlying

---

[1] Clay's *Annals of the Swedes*, pp. 143, 153–4.

[2] The original names were New Castle, Jones's, and Hoerekill, as it was called by the Dutch, or Deal.

province not yet given the privileges of a State. Instead of townships, the three Delaware counties were divided into "hundreds," an old Anglo-Saxon county method of division going back beyond the times of Alfred the Great. Delaware is the only State in the Union that retains this name for county divisions. The Three Lower Counties were allowed to send representatives to the Pennsylvania Assembly; and the Quakers of Delaware have always been part of the Yearly Meeting in Philadelphia.

In 1703, after having been a part of Pennsylvania for twenty years, the Three Lower Counties were given home rule and a legislature of their own; but they remained under the Governor of Pennsylvania until the Revolution of 1776. They then became an entirely separate community and one of the thirteen original States. Delaware was the first State to adopt the National Constitution, and Rhode Island, its fellow small State, the last. Having been first to adopt the Constitution, the people of Delaware claim that on all national occasions or ceremonies they are entitled to the privilege of precedence. They have every reason to be proud of the representative men they sent to the Continental Congress, and to the Senate in later times.

Agriculture has, of course, aways been the principal occupation on the level fertile land of Delaware; and it is agriculture of a high class, for the soil, especially in certain localities, is particularly adapted to wheat, corn, and timothy grass, as well as small fruits. That section of land crossing the State in the region of Delaware City and Middleton is one of the show regions in America, for crops of wheat and corn. Farther south, grain growing is combined with small fruits and vegetables with a success seldom attained elsewhere. Agriculturally there is no division of land of similar size quite equal to Delaware in fertility. Its sand and gravel base with vegetable mold above is somewhat like the southern Jersey formation, but it is more productive from having a larger deposit of decayed vegetation.

The people of Delaware have, indeed, very little land that is not tillable. The problems of poverty, crowding, great cities, and excessive wealth in few hands are practically unknown among them. The foreign commerce of Wilmington began in 1740 with the building of a brig named after the town, and was continued successfully for a hundred years. At Wilmington there has always been a strong manufacturing interest, beginning with the famous colonial flour mills at the falls of the Brandywine, and the breadstuffs industry at Newport on the Christina. With the Brandywine so admirably suited to the water-power machinery of those days and the Christina deep enough for the ships, Wilmington seemed in colonial times to possess an ideal combination of advantages for manufacturing and commerce. The flour mills were followed in 1802 by the Du Pont Powder Works, which are known all over the world, and which furnished powder for all American wars since the Revolution, for the Crimean War in Europe, and for the Allies in the Great War.

"From the hills of Brandywine to the sands of Sussex" is an expression the people of Delaware use to indicate the whole length of their little State. The beautiful cluster of hills at the northern end dropping into park-like pastures along the shores of the rippling Red Clay and White Clay creeks which form the deep Christina with its border of green reedy marshes, is in striking contrast to the wild waste of sands at Cape Henlopen. Yet in one way the Brandywine Hills are closely connected with those sands, for from these very hills have been quarried the hard rocks for the great breakwater at the Cape, behind which the fleets of merchant vessels take refuge in storms.

The great sand dunes behind the lighthouse at the cape have their equal nowhere else on the coast. Blown by the ocean winds, the dunes work inland, overwhelming a pine forest to the tree tops and filling swamps in their course. The beach is strewn with every type of wreckage of man's vain attempts to conquer the sea. The Life Saving Service men have strange tales to tell and show their collections of coins found along the sand. The old pilots live snugly in their neat houses in Pilot Row, waiting their turns to take the great ships up through the shoals and sands which were so baffling to Henry Hudson and his mate one hot August day of the year 1609.

The Indians of the northern part of Delaware are said to have been mostly Minquas who lived along the Christiana and Brandywine, and are supposed to have had a fort on Iron Hill. The rest of the State was inhabited by the Nanticokes, who extended their habitations far down the peninsula, where a river is named after them. They were a division or clan of the Delawares or Leni Lenapes. In the early days they gave some trouble; but shortly before the Revolution all left the peninsula in strange and dramatic fashion. Digging up the bones of their dead chiefs in 1748, they bore them away to new abodes in the Wyoming Valley of Pennsylvania. Some appear to have traveled by land up the Delaware to the Lehigh, which they followed to its source not far from the Wyoming Valley. Others went in canoes, starting far down the peninsula at the Nanticoke River and following along the wild shore of the Chesapeake to the Susquehanna, up which they went by its eastern branch straight into the Wyoming Valley. It was a grand canoe trip — a weird procession of tawny, black-haired fellows swinging their paddles day after day, with their freight of ancient bones, leaving the sunny fishing grounds of the Nanticoke and the Choptank to seek a refuge from the detested white man in the cold mountains of Pennsylvania.

BIBLIOGRAPHICAL NOTE

A LARGE part of the material for the early history of Pennsylvania is contained of course in the writings and papers of the founder. The *Life of William Penn* by S. M. Janney (1852) is perhaps the most trustworthy of the older biographies but it is a dull book. A biography written with a modern point of view is *The True William Penn* by Sydney G. Fisher (1900). Mrs. Colquhoun Grant, a descendant of Penn, has published a book with the title *Quaker and Courtier, the Life and Work of William Penn* (1907). The manuscript papers of Penn now in the possession of the Historical Society of Pennsylvania, together with much new material gathered in England, are soon to be published under the able editorship of Albert Cook Myers.

There is a vast literature on the history of Quakerism. The *Journal of George Fox* (1694), Penn's *Brief Account of the Rise and Progress of the People called Quakers* (1695), and Robert Barclay's *Apology for the True Christian Divinity* (1678) are of first importance for the study of the rise of the Society of Friends. Among the older histories are J. J. Gurney's *Observations on the Religious Peculiarities of the Society of Friends* (1824), James Bowden's *History of the Society of Friends in America*, 2 vols. (1850–54), and S. M. Janney's *History of the Religious Society of Friends*, 4 vols. (1860–67).

Two recent histories are of great value: W. C. Braithwaite, *The Beginnings of Quakerism* (1912) and Rufus M. Jones, *The Quakers in the American Colonies* (1911).

Among the older histories of Penn's province are *The History of Pennsylvania in North America*, 2 vols. (1797–98), written by Robert Proud from the Quaker point of view and of great value because of the quotations from original documents and letters, and *History of Pennsylvania from its Discovery by Europeans to the Declaration of Independence in 1776* (1829) by T. F. Gordon, largely an epitome of the debates of the Pennsylvania Assembly which recorded in its minutes in fascinating old-fashioned English the whole history of the province from year to year. Franklin's *Historical Review of the Constitution and Government of Pennsylvania from its Origin* (1759) is a storehouse of information about the history of the province in the French and Indian wars. Much of the history of the province is to be found in the letters of Penn, Franklin, Logan, and Lloyd, and in such collections as Samuel Hazard's *Register of Pennsylvania*, 16 vols. (1828–36), *Colonial Records*, 16 vols. (1851–53), and *Pennsylvania Archives* (1874–). A vast amount of material is scattered in pamphlets, in files of colonial newspapers like the *Pennsylvania Gazette*, in the publications of the Historical Society of Pennsylvania, and in the *Pennsylvania Magazine of History and Biography* (1877–). Recent histories of the province have been written by Isaac Sharpless, *History of Quaker Government in Pennsylvania*, 2 vols. (1898–99), and by Sydney G. Fisher, *The Making of Pennsylvania* (1896) and *Pennsylvania, Colony and Commonwealth* (1897). A scholarly *History of Proprietary Government in Pennsylvania* has been published by William R. Shepherd in the Columbia University *Studies* (1896) and the *Relations of Pennsylvania with the British Government, 1696–1765* (1912) have been traced with painstaking care by Winfred T. Root.

Concerning the racial and religious elements in Pennsylvania the following books contribute much valuable information: A. B. Faust, *The German Element in the United States*, 2 vols. (1909); A. C. Myers, *Immigration of the Irish Quakers into Pennsylvania, 1682–1750* (1902); S. W. Pennypacker, *Settlement of Germantown, Pennsylvania, and the Beginning of German Immigration to North America* (1899); J. F. Sachse, *The German Pietists of Provincial Pennsylvania, 1694–1708* (1895), and *The German Sectarians of Pennsylvania, 1708–1800*, 2 vols. (1899–1900); L. O. Kuhns, *The German and Swiss Settlements of Colonial Pennsylvania* (1901); H. J. Ford, *The Scotch-Irish in America* (1915); T. A. Glenn, *Merion in the Welsh Tract* (1896).

The older histories of New Jersey, like those of Pennsylvania, contain valuable original material not found elsewhere. Among these Samuel Smith's *The History of the Colony of Nova Cæsaria, or New Jersey* (1765) should have first place. E. B. O'Callaghan's *History of New Netherland*, 2 vols. (1846), and J. R. Brodhead's *History of the State of New York*, 2 vols. (1853, 1871) contain also information about the Jerseys under Dutch rule. Other important works are: W. A. Whitehead's *East Jersey under the Proprietary Governments* (New Jersey Historical Society *Collections*, vol. I, 1875), and "The English in East and West Jersey" in Winsor's *Narrative and Critical History of America*, vol. III, L. Q. C. Elmer's *The Constitution and Government of the Province and*

State of New Jersey (New Jersey Historical Society *Collections*, vols. III and VII, 1849 and 1872). Special studies have been made by Austin Scott, *Influence of the Proprietors in the Founding of New Jersey* (1885), and by H. S. Cooley, *Study of Slavery in New Jersey* (1896), both in the Johns Hopkins University *Studies;* also by E. P. Tanner, *The Province of New Jersey* (1908) and by E. J. Fisher, *New Jersey as a Royal Province, 1738–1776* (1911) in the Columbia University *Studies*. Several county histories yield excellent material concerning the life and times of the colonists, notably Isaac Mickle's *Reminiscences of Old Gloucester* (1845) and L. T. Stevens's *The History of Cape May County* (1897) which are real histories written in scholarly fashion and not to be confused with the vulgar county histories gotten up to sell.

The Dutch and Swedish occupation of the lands bordering on the Delaware may be followed in the following histories: Benjamin Ferris, *A History of the Original Settlements of the Delaware* (1846); Francis Vincent, *A History of the State of Delaware* (1870); J. T. Scharf, *History of Delaware, 1609–1888,* 2 vols. (1888); Karl K. S. Sprinchorn, *Kolonien Nya Sveriges Historia* (1878), translated in the *Pennsylvania Magazine of History and Biography*, vols. VII and VIII. In volume IV of Winsor's *Narrative and Critical History of America* is a chapter contributed by G. B. Keen on "New Sweden, or The Swedes on the Delaware." The most recent minute work on the subject is *The Swedish Settlements on the Delaware,* 2 vols. (1911) by Amandus Johnson.

INDEX

Academy of Natural Sciences founded, 60

Adams, John, on Quaker feasts, 31

Agriculture, in Pennsylvania, 25; in New Jersey, 156–58; on Cape May, 162; in Delaware, 226

Albany Treaty (1754), 88

American Philosophical Society, 58

Andros, Sir Edmund, Governor of New York, 134

Anne, Queen, colonial policy under, 44; Penn and, 74

Appoquinimink, Dutch at, 204

Aquidneck (Rhode Island), Quakers in, 7

Archdale, John, Governor of North Carolina, 7

Armstrong, Colonel John, 104–105

Attiqué, see Kittanning

Baltimore, Lord, 11; boundary dispute with Penn, 19, 24, 224

Baptists in Pennsylvania, 36

Barclay, Robert, Governor of East Jersey, 173; *Apology for the True Christian Divinity*, 173

Bartram, John, botanist, 57, 58

Bartram's Garden, Swedes build fort near, 208

Bates, William, Quaker immigrant, 139

Beekman, Dutch Governor in Delaware, 215

Beesley, *Sketch of Cape May*, quoted, 146 (note)

Belmont, country seat near Philadelphia, 33

Berkeley, Lord, Quakers buy West Jersey from, 6, 131; and New Jersey, 9, 129, 169

Berwyn, Welsh origin of name, 37

Black Minqua Indians (Eries), 207; see also Minqua Indians

Blackbeard, pirate, 208

Blackwell, Captain John, Governor of Pennsylvania, 68–69

Blue Anchor, tavern in Philadelphia, 28

Blue Bell tavern, 208

Bouquet, Colonel Henry, expedition, 109, 111

Bowden, James, *History of the Friends in America*, cited, 5 (note)

Braddock, General Edward, 95; defeat, 97–98

Bridgeton (N. J.), 148

Bridlington, old name for Burlington (N. J.), 136

Bright, John, 61

Brinser Brethren in Pennsylvania, 42

Brown, General Jacob, 61, 96

Brown's Mills (N. J.), 147

Bryn Mawr, Welsh origin of name, 37

Bucks County (Penn.), Quakers in, 55

Budden, Captain, brings chimes from England, 30